Knit (Spin) Sweden!

A Different Kind of Travel Book

Sara J. Wolf
Josefin Waltin

ISBN 13 (print): 978-1-937513-94-8

First edition
Published by http://www.cooperativepress.com

Photos provided by the authors are designated only by their initials
(SW or JW) and are copyrighted by them.

If you have questions or comments about this book, or need information about
licensing, custom editions, special sales, or academic/corporate purchases,
please contact Cooperative Press: info@cooperativepress.com or 10252 Berea Rd,
Cleveland, Ohio 44102 USA

For Cooperative Press
Senior Editor: Shannon Okey
Technical Editor: Andi Smith
Book Designer: Kim Richardson

*Title page: Oil painting of woman knitting, Emelia von Walterstorff, 1909.
Courtesy of Nordiska museet (NM.0191807), Bertil Wreting, Photographer*

Table of Contents

Table of Contents (cont.)

Introductions

SARA'S INTRODUCTION

Why a Travel Knitting/spinning Book? Why Sweden?

For many crafters, travel to another city or country is a great excuse to visit a local yarn shop and find a different yarn, a rare type of fleece, or a pattern that you've never seen before. If you're particularly lucky, you might happen on a meet-up and spend a glorious afternoon or evening knitting or spinning with new, instant friends. Traveling to another country multiplies the chances of not only finding something new, but for learning completely different techniques or styles of your craft.

Knitting, spinning, crochet, and many other crafts are not just for leisure entertainment and personal satisfaction. They were often done out of necessity, but now they are opportunities for life-long learning. They are avenues into other cultures, and insights into history. Although certainly helpful, you don't even need to learn another language (knitting has its own)…it's amazing how far you can go with such visual activities!

As a life-long knitter and traveler, I've sought to get beneath the surface of the places I've been lucky enough to visit. It has struck me over and over again that learning about a different culture not only opens your mind to new possibilities, but also gives you insight into different ways of thinking. Experiencing those differences lessens or removes that "otherness" that often is the source of misunderstanding. If we can better understand one another, we break down fear and prejudice.

On an organized tour, I'm probably a nightmare for the normal tour guide, since I always find another place I want to stop, photograph, and go to see. I've learned to travel on my own (and with Bruce) because I want to seek out those places that local artists and crafters find special, knit with the yarn of the local sheep, find a pattern for a traditional hat or sweater. This quest and my insatiable desire to learn new knitting techniques has led me here—to write this book for my fellow travelers as a starting point for their own special journey.

Of course I wasn't able to find every meet-up, festival, yarn shop or museum with historic knitted garments in their collection in Sweden, but I found quite a few. I leave it to all of you to expand on what I've done here. It is my goal to make my website (*aknitwizard.com*) a place to continue to collect information and changes to the marketplace in real time.

I would be remiss if I didn't call out some of the many people who helped me in my own journey through Sweden. Most important is my dear friend Karin Magnusson, someone I was lucky enough to work with 20 years ago at The Textile Museum in Washington, DC. Neither of us were good at remaining in touch, but on my first trip to Stockholm, she immediately volunteered as my travel guide, and we seemed to take off right from where we had left off so long ago—and our first stop was her local yarn shop. I came home with a bag full of Swedish yarn, and a strong desire to learn more about her beautiful country.

I dove into the Internet, and found things like a Festival of Mittens in the far north of Sweden near the Finnish border, and the lovely Monika Lund. Monika and the Norden Association of Pajala, organized the 6th annual festival in 2019 celebrating 100 years of the Lovikkavanten (Mitten of Lovikka) as a tribute to its inventor, Erika Aittamaa.

I stumbled on a *Threads* Magazine article from 1990 by Linda Sokalski on *tvåänds-stickning*—two end knitting (often referred to as "twined" knitting in English) that mentioned the craft school Sätergläntan run by the Swedish Handcraft Industries Association in the small town of Insjön in central Sweden. I was ready to sell everything I own and relocate until I could work my way through every class they offered, but settled on a one-week class on *tvåändsstickning* with the incomparable Karin Kahnlund. I was expecting a challenge—the class is taught in Swedish—but with patience and (much) laughter, was able to keep up and learn so much more than a new way to knit. Taking a knitting class in another country is truly a travel adventure!

When I discovered the depth of the subject of Swedish sheep—particularly the endangered breeds—I realized I was out of my depth, and appealed to Josefin Waltin, champion hand spinner, knitter, weaver and teacher, to help me navigate this complex but extremely interesting subject. Josefin blew apart many of my preconceived notions about spinning and forever widened my view of the world.

But why Sweden? Many of the people I interviewed wondered how I had chosen Sweden as a starting point. Surely the knitting of Norway was more famous, and what about Estonia with its amazing lace? Initially my answer had to do with a rather unpleasant experience. I had traveled with a group of knitters to various sites around the Baltic, and in each city, there was a mad scramble to get out and buy local yarns. As I watched the buying frenzy, I was disappointed to see that this was about acquisition, not understanding. Buying was the souvenir for the place, but it had no destination other than the knitter's stash. Nobody questioned the yarns' origins or what it might be best used for. Having worked for a time in a yarn store, I was very aware of the downside to impulse buys. Not quite enough for the sweater that would be "just perfect" from that yarn. Too fuzzy to make nice cables. Too scratchy to make a cowl to sit next to your neck. Not having a project in mind is often what leaves that special yarn in the closet. I asked some of the buyers about their plans, and the responses were almost always, "I don't really know, but I just want yarn that will be a memory of this place." A souvenir, but a sort of sad souvenir, particularly from Sweden, where a skein of one yarn might make a wonderful scarf, and another really should be felted or used as weft in a weaving to bring out its special nature.

So, the complexity of Swedish wool, and a lack of patterns in English (other than mostly for mittens) led me to dig deeper and deeper—to find the designers, to find the knitters and spinners, and to discover a place where so much was hidden just under the surface. Sweden has not only given me new insights into knitting history, but has given me many new friends that I hope to visit again and again. There is still so much to learn.

The list of people who helped me put all of this together is incredibly long, but special thanks go to:

- Sandy Zetterlund, Swedish Fibre, who took Bruce and me around western Sweden to meet shepherds, spinners and teachers, and introduced me to the wealth of fleece that she felt I should learn to spin.

- Josefin Waltin, not only my co-author and sage of fiber, but someone who was willing to make me answer hard questions, like why a travel book in an age where our every action has a potential or real impact on our earth's climate. Working with her has been an incredible and wonderful experience.
- Kate Isenberg, Karin Granström, Carina Olsson, and Jenny Bergström, Fårfest i Kil, for answering my endless questions, searching for resources, and cheering me on.
- Bo Runnberg and the members of the Föreningen Svenska Allmogefår for their generosity in allowing me to use their photographs of the special sheep breeds found only in Sweden.
- Monika Lund, for helping me with my research into knitting in the north, and locating links to pages on the internet that I would never have found on my own.
- Caroline Henkelius (Höner och Eir) for her long discussions and thoughtful emails that gave me real insight into the joys and difficulties of developing a wool-based business and restoring an old (and oftentimes unpredictable) spinning mill.
- Carina Nordahl for whispering translations in my ear when I got stuck in Karen Kahnlund's class.
- Marianne Larsson of the Nordiska Museet who so graciously opened the doors to their collections and gave me access to wonderful antique textiles to document and share with my readers.
- Lena Ideström at the Gotland Museum for allowing me to look at the incredible collection of Gotland knitting put together by Hermanna Stengård at the beginning of the 20th century.
- Helena Hassinsin, secretary of *Sticka!*, the Swedish Handknitting Guild for putting me in touch with local knitters in Stockholm and across the country, and the Retstickan group who immediately invited me to their monthly meet-up and Worldwide Knit in Public Day event.
- Four women who have been and continue to be my personal and professional extended family: Carolyn Rose, Sally Roy, Suzanne Larson and Melanie Pereira.
- My Wednesday knitting group at the Merriam-Gilbert Public Library who have no reason to read this book because they've already heard it in great detail as I worked my way through the research and writing. Thank you all for putting up with me!
- Last but not least, my thanks every day to Bruce for telling me I could do this, holding my hand every step of the way, and giving me a phenomenal garden in which to grow.

JOSEFIN'S INTRODUCTION

A Different Kind of Journey

Spinning is for me an inner journey. When I spin I give myself the gift of time to let my thoughts come and go, just as they are. All my thoughts and reflections are spun into the yarn and eventually the textile I make. My handspun projects thus contain all the memories of events and thoughts from the process of making. They also become maps of what I have learned along the way. These fibers have been through my hands numerous times from fleece to textile and from the texture I can find clues to where I stumbled upon a problem and what I learned from solving it.

When I travel to a new place I choose to do so on the ground. When I spin on the train the slowness of the making and traveling connect and reflect each other. The yarn I spin will forever remind me of that particular landscape.

The time it takes to prepare wool and spin, particularly on spindles, gives me time to learn and understand the wool, how it behaves and how it wants to be constructed to be its best yarn. I try to find the superpowers of this particular wool and let them shine in a yarn. Finding and enhancing the main characteristics of a wool is always my goal for both spinning and creating a textile.

I try to use local wool and work with a low carbon footprint. By going through all the steps of the process from raw fleece to a finished textile with hand tools I get a deeper understanding and appreciation of the time, love and skills behind handmade textiles through history. To me, working with a natural material like wool is a gift I thank my foremothers for.

Thanks to present wool heroes are in order too. First of all to Sara Wolf. If she hadn't invited me to this adventure I wouldn't have been writing this introduction at all. After having emailed and wool-mailed for six months we finally met. In a car. Going from Stockholm to the Kil sheep festival. Listening to Sara's talk in Kil made me so proud to be a part of the product and process that this book has become. This is only the beginning of our journey.

Wool oracle Kia Gabrielsson Beer who I call on our always open wool hotline with fiber conundrums. Kia has taught me so much and is a delight in the world.

Spin-Off magazine editor Kate Larson who encourages me to explore my writing and push my boundaries.

All shepherdesses who have provided me with fleece. I wouldn't have been able to participate in this book if it weren't for their love and care for their sheep. In the same spirit I thank all participating sheep for the gift of wool.

Students and followers who ask me questions that force me to investigate what I actually do. Thank you for teaching me how you learn.

Cecilia von Zweigbergk Wike, my dear friend. Cecilia helps me broaden my horizon and see the world from perspectives I didn't know existed.

Thank you to my family. My parents who encourage me in everything I do. Dan, my love and soul mate who supports me no matter what, asks the hard questions and helps prepare me for uncomfortable scenarios. Isak and Nora who smile with pride when I show them what I do and who grow up in a house with wool fiber in every corner and a faint but ubiquitous smell of sheep.

1 Knitting and Spinning in Sweden

There are many pitfalls to writing about early knitting history. For a start, archeology is always turning up new evidence that throws the information from previous publications out. For another, if you try to write about the craft of a country where theirs is not your first language, you are likely to put your foot into it. For those reasons, I'm not trying to make this a definitive history, but at the same time, am hoping I can share some of the traditions with you that I found so engaging and interesting.

In the scheme of things, knitting is a relative newcomer to the textile tradition. Long before it developed, hats, mittens, and stockings were constructed from flat fabric, or fashioned from nålbinding. This is true for Sweden as well as throughout Scandinavia, Europe and parts of the Middle East. Unlike knitting, nålbinding is created with a threaded needle, so only short lengths of wool can be used (drawing the full length of the wool through each stitch abrades the wool, so it would break quickly if the yarn was too long). Although sometimes called "needle knitting," nålbinding is actually a looping technique that is not related to knitting at all.

EARLY HISTORY

The oldest known nålbinding is believed to date to around 6500 BCE (from Nahal Hemar, Israel), and appears in Denmark around 4200 BCE. It was commonly used during the Viking age (793–1066 CE) for a variety of garments that were traded around the Baltic. The oldest known mitten in this technique in Sweden was found in Åsle and dates to about 200–300 CE Nålbinding is mentioned here not only because it is found and made at the same time that knitting began to be established, but because it is sometimes mistaken for knitting due to the shape of the stitches. While the craft began to die out once knitting became well established (knitting is much faster), it persisted in some parts of Sweden because of its durability, and like many handcrafts, has enjoyed renewed interest. You will find nålbound mittens along side knitted mittens and gloves (plain knitting, stranded knitting and two-end knitting) in museum collections throughout Sweden, and likewise will find classes taught in all of those techniques at various knitting shops.

≺ *Mitten in the nålbinding technique with embroidered designs*
Courtesy of Nordiska museet (NM.0248103), Mona-Lisa Djerf, photographer.

The development of knitting followed two paths: professional (workshop) knitting, and home knitting. There were professional knitting workshops in Spain and Italy at least as early as the 13th century but few objects remain from that time. The knitted items that exist are finely made and complex, making it difficult to guess how many years earlier the craft had started. All signs point to North Africa (Islamic regions) as well as Moorish Spain for earlier dates. That the Islamic community in those areas was the only group capable of producing the ultra-fine steel needles required for creating these items supports this theory.

There are a few pieces with known dates that help to provide a framework for knitting history. One of the earliest was found in the tomb of the Infante Fernando de la Cerda, who was buried in 1275 at the Abbey of Santa Maria la Real de Las Huelgas outside of Burgos, Spain. The edges of the cushion have the word "blessing" (baraka) knitted in Kufic script, indicating that this was most likely the work of mudéjar (Islamic) craftsmen. In his history of hand knitting, Richard Rutt notes that the cushion is knitted in stockinette stitch, at 80 sts/10 cm (or 20 sts/inch).[1]

The largest group of early knitted garments is liturgical gloves from across Europe. While some were cut and sewn from silk or linen fabric, many pairs were knit in fine silk with designs in silver and gilt thread. As with the Spanish cushion, these gloves were knit in workshops using extremely fine needles. It did not take long, however, for evidence to appear that showed knitting was not confined to guilds of male workers, but had found its way into women's hands.

Beautifully worked examples of stranded knitting can be found in the collections of museums like the Textile Museum in Washington, DC, dated between the 12th and 14th centuries. This sock (left) is one piece of knitting that convinces me that knitting started much earlier than the 12th century. With a complex series of operations to create the heel and the decreases at the toes, this wasn't a brand new craft. We may never know when it began, but I still daydream that I can time travel to where the first person figured out how to turn a heel and rejoice with them over that wonderful invention.

While we have yet to identify an early medieval knitted garment as originating from women who would have been working at home, there is a large body of religious art primarily from Italy showing Saint Mary knitting.

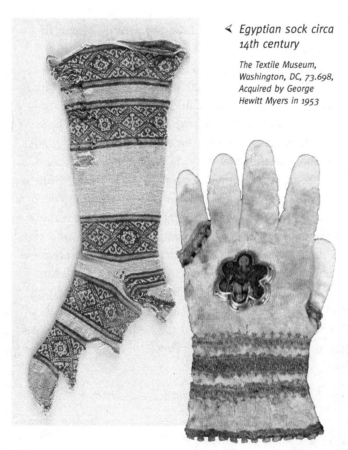

Three so-called "Knitting Madonnas" from Siena and Bologna date to between 1345 and 1355, and all show garments being knitted in the round on fine double-pointed needles. More famous than the early Italian examples is the Buxtehude Madonna (ca. 1400) by Master Bertram of Minden, who worked for many years in Hamburg.

We can't ascertain whether or not knitting was a significant activity nor if it was a practice for royalty or the general population. We don't know if it was having an increasing popularity for making garments, but it is significant that in the space of about 200 years, knitting had traveled from North Africa and Spain into Europe and Germany and was present in highly technical and skilled applications. But, could this textile craft have reached Sweden at such an early date? Here are a few intriguing ideas.

- The Vikings (late 8th to late 11th centuries) were not only great sailors, but great traders who made regular trips around the Baltic, and also had contact with Great Britain and as far as Constantinople. Among the caches of coins excavated from Spillings farm in northern Gotland are coins from 20 different nations, mainly in the Orient. These are dated to the year 870. Another from Burs parish (Gotland) contained 1441 Arabic coins, deposited in the mid-10th century.

- The Vikings were quickly supplanted by a federation of northern German cities around Lübeck to facilitate trade in the 12th century. This group became known as the Hanseatic League, with trading centers from Russia, through the Netherlands, Scandinavia and Britain. The near monopoly on trade in the Baltic was controlled through one such center on Gotland Island in Sweden.

- Knitted liturgical gloves appear throughout Europe with dates ranging from the 12th century (Prague, Czech Republic) to 16th century Spain, Italy and Germany[2].

- The earliest knitting guild in France was founded around 1268. By the early 16th century it was one of the six leading guilds of Paris with strict requirements as well as an exam to become a master knitter.[3]

- The first knitted caps in England come from the Coventry Cappers established in 1424 and records document women (Marjorie Claton of Ripon, Joan and Isabella Capper of Nottingham) were undertaking commercial knitting in 1465 and 1478 respectively.[4]

- While we have examples of knitted items from the 13th century that can be dated by their inclusion in a tomb, the next knitted garments with reliable dates do not occur until the mid-16th century. During his reign (1491-1547), Henry VIII launched his war ship *Mary Rose*, which almost immediately

◁ Cap recovered from the ship Mary Rose *which sank in 1545*

Knitted cap 81A3108 © The Mary Rose Trust

⋀ *Knitted scogger—arm or leg warmer, 1545*

Scogger 81A1936 ©The Mary Rose Trust

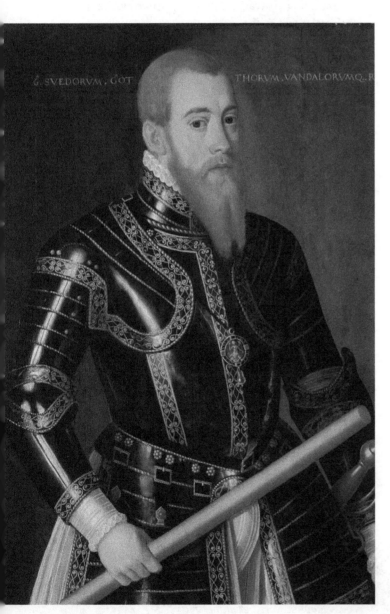

⋀ *Erik XIV (1533-1577) attributed to Domenicus Verwilt*

Nationalmuseum #18413, public domain

sank off the English coast in 1545. Three complete knitted hats were preserved along with a scogger (used either as a sleeve or on the lower leg like a leg warmer). The Monmouth Caps originating in Wales, were commonly worn by soldiers and sailors, and were knitted and felted by men from the Weaver's Guild.

- The scogger recovered from the *Mary Rose* is interesting for a couple of reasons. First, the leg (or arm) covering continued to be used long after knitted socks and stockings were becoming more common, and in fact didn't replace knitwear completely in colder climates where sewn leg wrappings continue to be used into the 19th century.[5] Nevertheless, there are sufficient fragmentary knitted items from Tallin, Estonia dating from the 15th century to indicate a widespread use of knitting.[6]

There are a few items found so far in Sweden that suggest that knitting was already a well-established textile craft by the time of Erik XIV (1533-1577). King Erik pursued Elizabeth I of England in spite of her 1560 letter to him indicating a lack of interest. He even departed for England to attempt an in-person appeal for her hand. A storm prevented him reaching his goal, and he came home without Elizabeth, but apparently with a pair of silk stockings—his 1566 wardrobe inventory included at least 27 pairs in addition to those made of fabric and leather (unfortunately these didn't survive).[7]

What did survive from Erik's reign is a glove that can be found today in the Treasury of Uppsala Cathedral. In 1565, Sten Svantesson Sture, captain of the warship *Svansen* perished during a battle against the Danes and Lübeckers. His clothing was laid in the family chapel in Uppsala Cathedral, including a black felt hat with a small knitted glove attached. The glove was worked in narrow bands of color, and finger rings were simulated by bands of gold thread. Across the palm are the words

< Knitted glove,
possibly from
Germany, dated
to 1565 and the
death of Sten
Svantesson Sture

Sture Glove courtesy
Uppsala Cathedral,
Anders Tukler,
Photographer

➤ Tvåändsstickage glove
from Born foundry
(Dalarna Province),
mid-late 16th century

Courtesy of the Dalarnas
Museum (DM18966), Fredrik
Hegert, Photographer

FREVHEN SOFIA. It is believed that Sten was betrothed to a German girl with the name Sofia, and that the glove had been attached to the hat as a favour. By this date she probably would have been the knitter.

Archeological excavations are one way we continue to fill in the gaps of knitting history. While fabrics are rarely preserved, the few fragments we find continue to build our knowledge, while also raising more questions. Among the artifacts excavated from Born (Dalarna Province) was a glove worked in tvåändsstickning (two-end knitting). To date, this is the earliest example of this technique in Scandinavia. With a carbon-14 date of 1550-1600, it becomes that much more certain that a very sophisticated level of knitting had become commonplace in Sweden by the mid-16th century, for this certainly was *not* workshop production. In fact, Sweden never did develop a professional guild system for knitting.

From the 16th century forward, as home knitters produced hats, gloves, mittens and socks for their families, knitting also became an important component of the economy. One of the most commonly cited references for early domestic knitting comes from Susanne Pagolith's book *Nordic Knitting*. She notes that in Halland (part of Denmark until 1645) Magna Brita Cracau, a Dutch woman, and her servants taught knitting to the people on the Vallens estate in Växtorp sometime during the 1650s. Not only could the tenants pay their taxes with knitting, the financial reward was sufficient that wool had to be imported from Denmark and Iceland to support this burgeoning cottage industry.[8] This has been quoted over time as the earliest evidence of knitting in Sweden, but clearly that is not the case as archeology conclusively shows.

At the same time as the Halland example, the wealthy imported finely knitted silk garments from workshops in Italy into Sweden and other parts of Scandinavia. Some of the commerce was driven by the rapid transit of fashion via the fashion doll (also known as Pandora Dolls).

> Pandora Doll
> circa 1600 owned
> by Christina of
> Holstein-Gottorp
>
> Courtesy of
> Livrustkammaren
> (Royal Armoury
> Museum), Stockholm

⋏ Silk knitted waistcoat worn by Charles I
of England at his execution in 1649

Collection of the Museum of London

Knitted garments have not been found on any of these dolls to date, but this doll, sent to Christina from a relative in the Spanish court, shows how easily fashion traveled from one region to another. And, while gowns with gilt lace may have been restricted to certain classes, nothing stopped imitation. Another reason these dolls may not exhibit knitted garments is that the garment that seems to have been copied and transformed by all classes, was the knitted waistcoat—an undergarment.

The waistcoat originally was a garment like an undershirt—pulled over the head and worn for warmth. Often knitted in fine silk, and sometimes padded with strands of silk fiber for extra insulation, these garments were so expensive and valuable that they were cut and re-sewn as fashions changed, and handed down to others as long as they could be repaired and reused.

Records from a merchant of Malmö dated to 1598 indicate that these garments were being imported and remained popular into the 17th century.[9]

One example of a waistcoat that remained in its original form is the shirt that Charles I of England wore to his execution in January 1649. It was said that his garment choice was made so that he wouldn't shiver from the cold and appear to be afraid.

Two 17th century waistcoats are preserved in Swedish museums, one in the Nordiska Museum in Stockholm, and another in the Goteborgs Stadsmuseum (Gothenburg City Museum). This second garment, altered to open in the front, is a beautiful example of damask-knit style with a raised pattern. Knit in the round, the waistcoat from Goteborgs Stadsmuseum has two purl stitches at each side in imitation of the side seam.

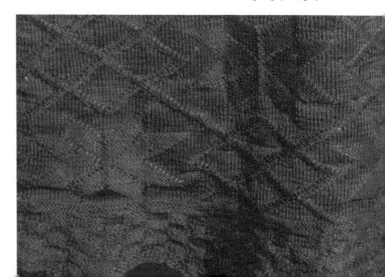

LINING WITH THRUMS

Insulation added to garments in the form of yarn (spun or unspun) is typically known as "thrums." The term comes from the name for the warp yarn left on the loom after the fabric has been cut off. These lengths of yarn are too short for most applications, but thrifty individuals realized that the yarn could be used to add insulation to hats, socks and mittens. There is no clear evidence that the idea came from this 17th century application to waistcoats, but that is one of the earliest examples we see of this kind of insulating fiber being used. Maj Ringgard has identified several damask-knitted waistcoats in collections in Denmark (as well as the Goteborgs Stadsmuseum example) that feature either knitted-in or knotted-in strands of silk.[10]

Thrums also were used on the outside of caps to render them water resistant. This illustration of an English sailor (late 16th/early 17th century) shows a thrummed hat. These hats were knitted and felted, with the thrums being either knitted in or knotted in later (after fulling).

The English thrummed caps for sailors were sufficiently common that you will find references to them in Elizabethan songs like, *The Ballad of the Caps*.

> The Monmouth Cap, the Saylors' Thrum,
> And that wherein the Tradesmen come;
> The Physick lawe, the Cap divine,
> And that which crowns the muses nine;
> The Cap that fools do countenance,
> The goodly Cap of Maintenance.
>
> Any Cap, whate'er it be, Is still the sign
> of some degree.
>
> The Souldiers that the Monmouth wear,
> On castle tops their Enseignes rear:
> The Saylors with their Thrums do stand
> On higher place than all the land.
>
> Any Cap whate'er it be, is still the sign of some degree.[11]

The literal translation of vattenbärarvantar is "water-carrier mittens," and it certainly makes sense that thrums would be ideal as insulation for someone carrying a bucket of water in the cold. They remain popular to this day, with thrums of yarn (pulled; never cut from a ball of yarn) or fleece/roving knitted into the mitten fabric.

A pattern for making thrummed mittens can be found on page 140.

⋀ *Vattenbärarvantar from Värmland courtesy of Carina Olssen*

Öyvind Lund, Photographer

⋀ *English sailor in a thrummed hat*

Habiti Antichi e Moderni by Cesare Vecelli, 1598, public domain

∧ *Tröja from Skåne, 1830-1850. Note the resemblance of the knitted star pattern in this sweater to the Gothenburg 17th century waistcoat. Also, the overall sweater shape with a curved neckline and fairly straight sleeve inset is also reminiscent of the 17th century style.*

©Nordiska museet (NM.0131653), Mona-Lisa Djerf, photographer

Many of the traditional regional sweaters in Sweden (some of which originally were worn as under garments) resemble the waistcoat design closely. There are examples both of those pulled over the head, and those with front openings.

The sweater type that most closely resembles the Italian damask-knit waistcoats of the 17th century is this type from Skåne in southern Sweden.

This tröja from Hälsingland (below) is also a design that was originally worn as an undergarment.

⊰ *Tröja with distinctive patterns of Hälsingland, and the date 1876 knitted below the neckline. This sweater has the same basic shape as both the waistcoat and the Skåne sweater*

©Nordiska museet (0157270), Mona-Lisa Djerf, photographer

The traditional jackets of Dalarna Province are similar
to the open-front style that evolved from the 17th century
Italian waistcoats. Here the body of the jacket is a woven
and embroidered fabric, and the sleeves are worked in
tvåändsstickning. Many sleeves from this region were
knit in white yarn with black patterning, and then dyed
red after the knitting was completed.

In the 19th century a different technique began to
appear across Germany, Estonia and Scandinavia.
Näverstickning (known in English as entrelac) may
have come from Germany, as the earliest examples in
museum collections date to between 1810-1830 originated
in Germany. With examples collected on Gotland Island
and in Estonia also dating to the late 19th/early 20th
century, that certainly
is a reasonable conjec-
ture since Germany
and Sweden were
close trading partners.
However, documen-
tary evidence is still
lacking.

The name of this knitting technique in Swedish—näverstickning—comes from the word näver for birch bark. Traditional birch bark baskets resemble the shapes of the knitted entrelac squares.

There also is the thought that the technique may have come into Sweden via Lappland and/or Jämtland with people known as the Forrest Finns. Both routes into northern Sweden are equally plausible. The result was inclusion of this technique during the late 19th and early 20th century on stockings, mittens, and sometimes leggings.

Knee-high stockings worked in entrelac were collected in Gällivare and Jukkasjärvi (northern Sweden) and are documented in Erika Falck's Book *Fancy Mittens*.[12] While contemporary knitters have revived its use, it is not a technique that gained wider appeal internationally until the late 20th century. Although it was used throughout Scandinavia, Estonia and Germany, there are no examples of entrelac in the many 19th century pattern books printed in English. This includes reviews of the hundreds of books in the University of Southampton Library donated by knitting historian Richard Rutt or in similar knitting books published in the United States.[13]

The late 19th century also produced one of the most iconic mittens of Sweden—the Lovikka mitten. Created by Erika Aittamaa (1866–1952) from Lovikka village, this mitten was made for a cart driver (forböndern) wishing to have a hearty, hardwearing and waterproof mitten that

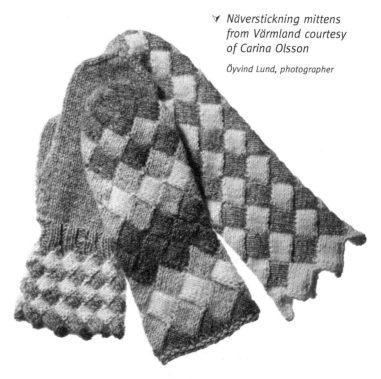

would last several winters. Erika spun a thick yarn and made her mitten on needles small enough to create a very dense fabric. Her first attempt did not win acclaim, and in fact, her client told her she had ruined the wool. But her next pair, which she brushed with a steel comb to raise the nap and carefully washed, was accepted. This mitten became very popular not only with the forböndern, but with the general population as well. They were, in fact, sufficiently popular to provide her a living. After making some plain, she began adding embroidery at the cuff, and that style enjoyed an even greater popularity.

These mittens regained popularity when Sweden's Princess Sibylla wore a pair on a ski trip in 1933. The Princess' photo in newspapers wearing the mittens provided a boost to the economy for knitters during the depression years of the 1930s.

◄ *Erika Aittamaa, creator of the Lovikka mitten (circa 1930)*

⋀ *Fragments of näverstickning*

From the collection of Gotlands Hemslöjdsförening. SW photo.

In 1962, the Lovikka Husmodersförening (Housewife Association) received a patent for these mittens, ensuring that only the mittens from that village, made of hand spun wool, knitted, washed, brushed and embroidered by hand, receive the seal of the Lovikka brand. Still, most knitters in Sweden knit this style of mitten as one of their first projects. While some use two or 3 strands of unspun wool, many are made from commercial Lovikka-style yarn produced by several Swedish spinning mills and sold in many knitting shops.

The Industrial Revolution occurred later in Sweden than in England and some other parts of Europe, but by the end of the 19th century, both the wool and linen industries had collapsed. This didn't mean that spinning, kitting and weaving wasn't still an important component of home life, but that gradually less expensive commercially made garments and household goods began to replace some of those that were homemade. In fact, even though handcrafts were widely taught as part of the school curriculum, many urban Swedes looked upon crafts as things only done by the poor. In at least two locations, however there were teachers who recognized the value of traditional knitting and design, and made it their mission to save whatever they could, and document what remained for the future.

Hermanna Stengård, an elementary school teacher born in 1861, saw the decline of knitting on Gotland Island and began collecting patterns and worn out examples of knitted garments to preserve the design heritage. In addition to the knitting, she also collected folk histories and folk tales that she made into a book, published in 1925, entitled *Gotländsk Sticksöm Gamla Mönster* (republished as a facsimile edition in 2014 by Bokförlaget Rediviva). In the 1984 translation of *The Mitten Book*, Inger and Ingrid Gottfridsson quoted Hermanna Stengård as follows, "To all old knitting artists who live here, to those who cherish the traditional art of Gotland as a valuable jewel, and to all who appreciate keeping this art, I make a warm appeal not to weary. Let us help each other to save the scraps so they are not wasted."[14]

It was an incredible privilege to see these "scraps" in person. In addition to the knitted samples, the collection contains several small notebooks with samples and Hermanna's notes.

Other samples from the collection owned by the Gotlands Hemslöjdsförening include fragments of socks and mittens, a small sampler and a knee-length Entrelac stocking that is nearly identical to one from a similar time period from Lappland. The stocking in the collection is not the same as the one pictured in Hermanna's

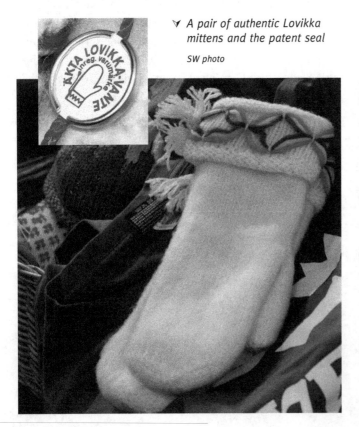

⊻ *A pair of authentic Lovikka mittens and the patent seal*

SW photo

◁ *Hermanna Stengård*

Public domain

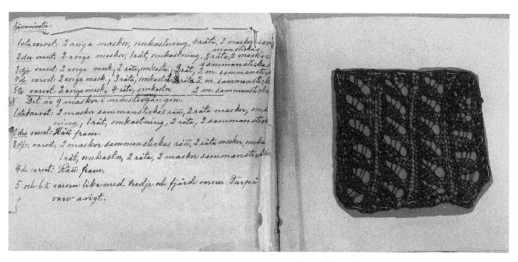

One of Hermanna
Stengård's notebooks
documenting knitting
patterns on Gotland Island

*Materials from Hermanna
Stengård's collection, courtesy
of Gotlands Hemlöjdsförening.
SW photos*

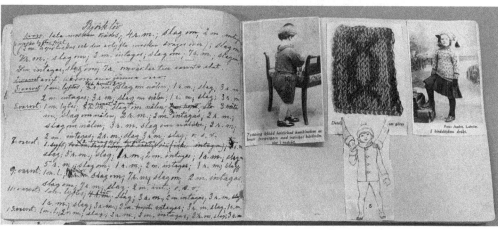

Hermanna Stengård's
instructions for lace

*Materials from Hermanna
Stengård's collection, courtesy
of Gotlands Hemlöjdsförening.
SW photos*

Knitted fragments collected
by Hermanna Stengård

*Materials from Hermanna
Stengård's collection, courtesy
of Gotlands Hemlöjdsförening.
SW photos*

◁ Teres Torgrim and her students, early 20th century

Norrländska Socialdemokraten newspaper, photographer unknown

Another teacher—Teres Torgrim—began collecting mittens in the Jukkasjärvi area in Norrbotten County north of the Arctic Circle. One of the last nomad school teachers, Teres not only taught children the academic subjects, she also taught both boys and girls to knit, using patterns collected from the region.

Designs collected by Teres Torgrim are featured in Erika Falck's book *Fancy Mittens. Stickat från Norrbotten* by Marika Larsson is another collection of patterns from that region.

In 1947 during repairs to the Jukkasjärvi Church, a number of well-preserved graves were found under the floor. Sitting beside the open graves, Teres copied two patterned mittens from the many knitted garments found there. These include the fingerless mitt in natural wool colors from the photo below as well as a natural/white mitten with raised designs at the cuff shown on the next page.

At the time of the excavation, the mitten Teres produced was knit in ordinary stockinette stitch with purl stitch decorations at the cuff. Later she made additional reproduction mittens based on the white mitten from

book, suggesting that her collection may well have been larger at one time.

Hermanna need not have worried, as the knitters on Gotland Island (and elsewhere) continue to use her designs and adapt them to many projects. At the Yllet shop in Visby, Frida Asplund has been working a long sampler of these designs to help knitters visualize how they might be used with different yarns and at a different scale (page 83). They also can be found on mittens and hats in craft shops not only in Gotland, but also across Sweden.

◁ Designs from Jukkasjärvi area

Courtesy of Erika Falck, Kasja Tuolja, photographer

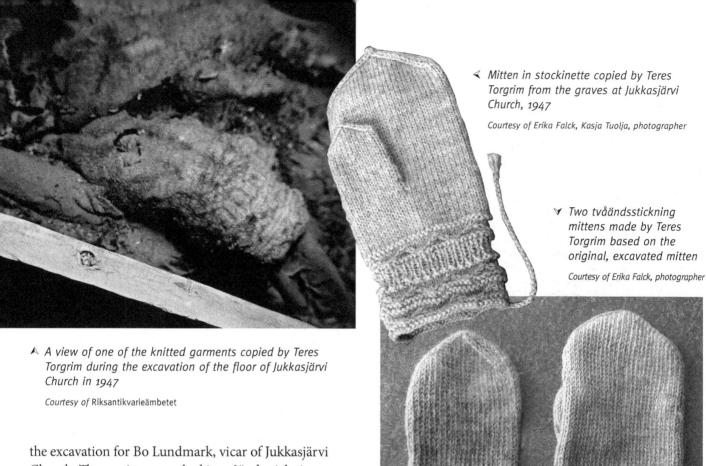

the excavation for Bo Lundmark, vicar of Jukkasjärvi Church. These mittens worked in tvåändsstickning, are likely Teres' later attempt to reproduce those mittens in the correct technique.

KNITTING IN THE 20TH CENTURY

Perhaps because spinning and knitting have been such an integral aspect of home life, I have not found that much written (at least in English) about knitting in the early 20th century. There are, however, enough photographs in museums and archives to document the important place of knitting in Swedish culture.

Perhaps the best-known example of the influence of knitting on Swedish commerce began in 1939 with the establishment of *Bohus Stickning* in Gothenburg. What started as an economic relief project for the wives of

In 1998, Solveig Gustafsson was asked to try to reproduce some of the Bohus knitting patterns. With thorough research and careful control of the dyeing process, new pattern kits were developed. Solveig was every bit as much of a perfectionist as Emma Jacobsson had been, and Bohus Stickning was reborn.

When Solveig decided to retire in 2013, news spread immediately and the entire stock of pattern kits at the museum was sold out (mainly to American knitters who had quick access to the internet). Pernille Silfverberg, an angora farmer nearby had the same spirit of perfectionism, and she became the new keeper of the tradition. Working with Henrichsens Uldspinderi, a 5th generation family spinning mill in Denmark, the very special wool/angora yarn continues to be produced under Permille's supervision, and the Museum is able to continue to sell Bohus Stickning patterns and kits.

By the 1960s there was a downturn in interest in knitting due to the ready availability of cheaper machine-knit goods. At the same time the increase in the number of women working outside of the home limited time availability to practice traditional crafts. Ironically, very soon in the 1970s craft and tradition suddenly had an international revival. It is important to note, though, that knitting had never disappeared from Sweden's homes or educational landscape.

unemployed quarrymen became a thriving business providing exceptionally high-quality sweaters to the wealthy elite in Europe and the United States. Movie stars like Ingrid Bergman and Grace Kelly wore these expensive and highly coveted garments. Company founder, Emma Jacobsson very carefully controlled the quality of the wool and product design, adding to the mystique of these garments.

During WWII, there was a shortage of wool, so Bohus Stickning yarn was augmented by angora, which contributed not only to the luxury of the yarn, but to the soft "halo" effect that became one of the hallmarks of Bohus garments.

In the 1940s, as many as 3-4,000 sweaters were sold in a year, but by the 1960s, styles were changing to such a degree that sales declined steadily and the company closed in 1969.[15]

⊳ *The sweater, hat, and glove kits still produced for sale by the Bohusläns Museum involve careful precision of yarn and dye production, using the same color cards developed under Emma Jacobsson's supervision in the 1930s. "Blue Shimmer" designed by Anna-Lisa Mannheimer-Lunn*

Courtesy of the Bohusläns Museum (UM031462)

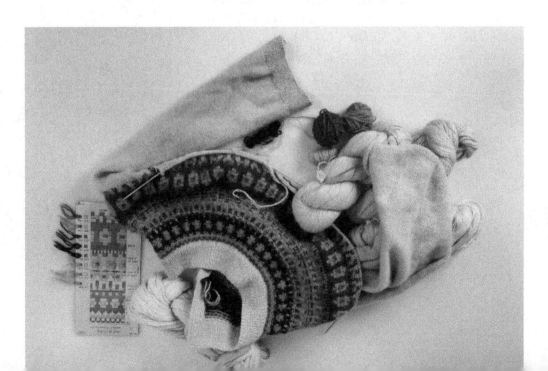

LIFELONG LEARNING

There are a large number of opportunities to learn all of the traditional crafts in Sweden—hampered only by ones abilities with the language. It is definitely worth mentioning crafts education, however, because craft and learning craft are such an integral component of Swedish culture. While there is sometimes a tendency to think of crafting as things we "used to do," schools in Sweden made a concerted effort to keep traditional components of everyday life from earlier centuries embedded in compulsory education beginning at the age of 6.

Slöjd or "craft/handicraft" (including woodwork, metal crafting paper-folding, sewing, embroidery, knitting, crochet and weaving) has been a part of school curriculum in Sweden since the 1870s. The teaching methods begun by Uno Cygnaeus in Finland in 1865 were promoted by Otto Salomon in Sweden beginning in the 1870s. This educational component was considered important to building character as well as manual dexterity and industriousness. It also went along with the need to extend arts education at a time when craft guilds were ending. The end of guilds occurred at the beginning of the 19th century, and the industrial revolution and globalization ushered in the decline of domestic crafts. The *Nääs Method* developed by Salomon persisted well into the 20th century, and has undergone many modifications. What remains fundamental to this concept is the idea that education should be based on a child's imagination and play.[16]

⋏ *Summer class at Säterglätan Institute*

SW photo

One big change for knitting came when the knitting method changed from carrying the yarn in the right hand (English-style or throwing) to carrying the yarn in the left hand (European/Continental, or picking) to improve efficiency and speed. Where the tradition of tvåändsstickning persisted, knitters have had to be ambidexterous working with the yarn in their right hand in order to twist the yarn between stitches.[17]

Crafts education in the schools has its ups and downs in terms of popularity and effectiveness. Like arts programs in many countries, there often is an eye towards reducing them when funds are tight. There is less of an emphasis on the importance of teacher education for crafts teaching, creating unevenness in the quality of instruction. Some knitters expressed that as they had developed their interest in knitting, it was sometimes criticized as something "only poor people do." Nonetheless, the craft tradition remains strong, with children continuing to be exposed to crafts in school, and through the government's continued support of handicrafts coordinators in every region.

In addition, the non-profit Hemslöjdden (National Association of Swedish Handicraft Societies https://hemslojden.org/) includes both regional and local handicraft societies offering courses, exhibitions, publications and scholarships to promote crafts education, and acts as the trade body issuing journeyman licenses and craftsperson certificates in the professions of hand weaving, knitting, embroidery, woodwork, and pottery. The Association also is a trustee of Säterglätan Institute for Handicrafts, a residential school for post-graduate craft education. Säterglätan also offers week-long summer courses in a range of subjects.

Across the country you also will find a range of local institutions organized as centers of continuing education, with opportunities for individuals to complete secondary education if they have left school, or for those wanting to expand their education into other areas. These schools have been founded by benevolent societies, trade unions, political entities and regional governmental organizations all as a way of spreading knowledge and culture. These schools very often offer short summer courses of a week, or weekend courses in crafts.

For the casual visitor, this range of educational opportunities that are available for all ages, seem to be just out of reach. Participation usually requires the ability to be sufficiently fluent in Swedish to comprehend the technical parameters of the crafts. Since many of the teachers at these schools speak English, however, there could be opportunities to arrange special classes for small groups working through the regional schools, the regional handicrafts specialists, or the knitting shops.

 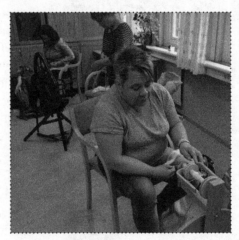

⋏ *Button sculpture outside school building (left), 3-day summer class—spinning workshop conducted by Anna Josefsson (who is also the school's biology teacher in Västra Götland County on the west coast of Sweden) (right).*

SW photo

KNITTING IN THE 21ST CENTURY

Like everywhere else, interest in knitting and spinning in Sweden ebbs and flows. In recent years, knitting shops have increased in numbers and then just as suddenly closed. The same can be said for spinning mills. Some of the larger and more established mills that closed within the last 20 years have been reopened by new entrepreneurs. They hope to take advantage of the surge in interest in heritage breeds and fuel a drive to produce more environmentally friendly, sustainable products. Still, with a poor market for wool, many small farms and shepherds with small conservation flocks struggle to survive.

After Radio Sweden's 2015 report that an estimated 75% of wool was either being burned or composted for lack of a market, interest in Swedish wool improved. However, there is a strong tension between the desire to keep the traditions going, and the lack of profitability of wool production. Yet, with the number of breeds and the amazing variety of wool fiber types, there is huge potential. Developing a system to provide a consistent supply of Swedish fleece and wool will determine the success of turning this small industry from a mainly internal and limited activity to an international market. The other system that currently is lacking in Sweden is a standard grading system for fleece. It clearly will take both time, and aggressive marketing to compete on the international stage.

Depending on who you ask, you may find some Swedes thinking that interest in knitting is waning, particularly among young adults. This was the opinion of at least one of the Stockholm shop owners I interviewed, who felt that her client demographic is primarily women who no longer have children at home and are picking up knitting again now that they have more free time. There are quite a few folks who would disagree, however, including women of all ages who regularly meet up to knit at Knit Cafés (Stick Kafe). On an early June evening, the Retstickan group pictured here met at Café Ritorno in Odenplan, as they do regularly.

Knitters and some crocheters of a variety of ages and abilities insisted that knitting get-togethers continue to increase in numbers and locations. One knitter said that within the Stockholm area it was possible to find a different group to knit with nearly every day of the month. This particular group also regularly meets up for World Wide Knit in Public Day (generally the first weekend in June).

The Retstickan group is one of dozens that are loosely affiliated by the Swedish knitting guild association *Sticka!* (*https://www.sticka.org/*) That group, open to anyone interested in knitting, provides a means of communication for locals to meet up and also for visitors to another city to find like-minded individuals to knit with for an afternoon or evening. Various groups also plan trips and workshops, and some shops across the country provide discounts to *Sticka!* members. The organization, with a small volunteer board (and minimal annual dues), maintains a website with a calendar of meet-ups and fiber events throughout Sweden, as well as a Facebook page and Ravelry group.

Many knitting shops also sponsor periodic knit cafés, although they are not widely publicized and you may need to ask at various shops to find one. Some, but not all shops post notices on their websites for meet-ups.

⋏ *WWKIP June 2019, Stockholm*

SW photo

⋏ Sticka! *group Retstickan at Café Ritorno in 2019*

Bruce Nappi, photographer

One way that Swedes are creating knitting interest is through the output of their many, creative designers. Some, like Elsabeth Lavold, are already widely known. Others have a strong following in Europe and Scandinavia. The social media site Ravelry is also serving as a platform to bring new, young designers to the attention of an international audience. These designers find inspiration from the roots and traditions of Swedish craft, but also are moving into very interesting, contemporary fashion that has impact well beyond their borders. We can only guess at what might be next!

SPINNING

You could think of spinning as the Mother of textile crafts. It predates weaving; itself at least 27,000 years old, according to recent work by Professor Olga Soffer of the University of Illinois[18]. A more recent discovery in a rock shelter in southern France indicates that spun fibers were in use at least 41,000 to 52,000 years ago. This discovery, of a 3-ply cord used to attach a worked stone to a handle (a tool) wasn't just a bunch of fibers twisted together. Rather, it was a deliberate manufacture of cordage, with three fiber bundles twisted counterclockwise, and those twisted bundles twisted together clockwise to form the cord.[19]

Early cordage, string, or yarn, need not have been spun in the manner we think of today, using a spindle—it easily could have been twisted by hand—but evidence of spindle whorls is found in archeological sites around the world by 3,000 to 6,000 years ago in China and in Neolithic Europe as early as 12,000 years ago. By the time of the earliest settlements in Sweden, weaving was well established, and we have enough fragmentary evidence to understand quite a bit about the clothing made and worn throughout Scandinavia.

Spinning, weaving, and ultimately, knitting, were activities of necessity in nearly every household in Sweden. Commercial spinning mills didn't really provide "competition" to home-based hand spinning until the 19th century and the rise of industrialization, and even then, spinning, knitting and weaving continued to be an important component of Swedish daily life.

Hand spinning, like other crafts, has enjoyed a boost from the current widespread interest in sustainability as well as the ingrained Swedish cultural appreciation of traditional arts. Spinning classes can be found not only at the craft high schools and through local shops and craft weekends, but are a regular feature of the summer program at post-secondary educational schools like Sätergläntan Institute.

Nowhere is the interest in fleece and spinning more evident than at the annual Swedish fleece and spinning championships (Ull I Kubik) began in 2011, and co-sponsored in 2019 by the non-profit Ullvilja Association and Öströö Fårfarm. The purpose of Ullvilja is to promote and develop wool processing with an emphasis on Swedish wool.

⋏ *Weaving and wool carding in early 20th century Sweden*

Courtesy of the Bohusläns Museum (UMFA53464_0521 and UMFA53464_02299), Johan Johansson, photographer

The championships are extremely challenging and have a different emphasis each year. Entrants receive fleece for their category (intermediate or advanced) a few weeks before the competition, and must return the finished product by a specified date for evaluation and judging.

The advanced category in 2019 used archeological textiles from the Varberg Museum as inspiration. The so-called "Bockstan Man" (Bockstensmannen) is the remains of a medieval body found in a bog in Varberg Municipality, dating to between 1290 and 1430. The bog preserved a great deal of the man's clothing, including his shirt, a woolen cloak, and a gugel hood. His legs were even covered by a type of hosiery.

The challenge for the spinners was to produce a warp and a weft yarn inspired by Bockstan Man's cloak, from the raw wool of *Värmland* sheep.

➢ Illustration of a gugel hood

Illustration from Wikimedia Commons

⩔ Reproductions of medieval clothing found in a bog in Varberg Municipality dating to between 1290 and 1430

Charlotta Sandelin/Hallands kulturhistoriska museum

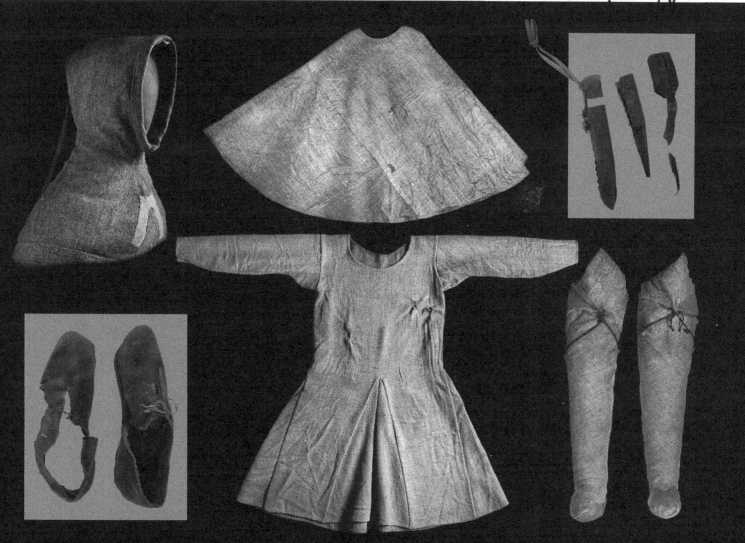

Josefin Waltin, a gold metal winning spinner, separated the locks by color, and then mixed the colors and white by plying them together.

The weft yarn she submitted was a singles yarn spun on a Navajo spindle.

The 2019 intermediate level required spinners to submit a cable-plied sock yarn from *Gute* lamb fleece.

While we live in a world that is very different than that of Bockstensmannen, life's complexity and pace make it likely that we will continue to turn to our foundations

∀ Josefin's preparation of warp and weft yarns inspired by the Bockstan Man's cloak for the 2019 Uil I Kubik spinning competition.

⅄ Värmland *wool: mixed white, brown and grey*

JW photos

⅄ *Worsted outer coat singles ready to be plied*

⅄ *Finished lace-weight (265m/kg) warp yarn*

⅄ *Finished singles weft yarn (4335 m/kg)*

⅄ *The competing weaving yarns in the advanced category*

for inspiration and peace in the midst of confusion. The feel of fleece sliding through our fingers and becoming yarn; the rhythmic click of needles making warm clothing, are touchstones not only to our past, but also to our inner core. Exploration may start at home, but we extend our knowledge through the gift of similar crafts from other lands. Join the adventure, and knit (and spin) Sweden.

⌄ *Preparation of cable-plied sock yarn from* Gute *fleece.*

⌃ *This fleece has extremely fine fibers but also lots of black kemp*

JW photos

⌃ *Flicking and carding removed most of the kemp. The remainder will work itself out eventually*

⌃ *Finished fingering weight cable-plied yarn*

⌃ *Competing sock yarns in the intermediate category*

FOOTNOTES

1. Rutt, Richard. *A History of Hand Knitting*. London, B.T. Batsford Ltd., 1987. p. 40.

2. Tribe, Shawn. *Pontifical Gloves: A Brief History and Consideration*, 17/7/2018 Liturgical Arts Journal https://www.liturgicalartsjournal.com/2018/07/pontifical-gloves-brief-history-and.html

3. Turnau, Irena. *History of Knitting Before Mass Production*, 1991, Warsaw, Institute of the History of Material Culture, Polish Academy of Sciences.

4. Rutt, op cit. p 58

5. Pink, Anu, *Estonian Knitting II, Socks and Stockings*, 2018, Türi, Saara Publishing House, p 10.

6. Pink, op cit, pg 16

7. Ekstrand, Gudrun. Some early silk stockings in Sweden, *Textile History* 13(2), 1982, pp165-182.

8. Pagolith, Susanne. *Stickat från Norden*. 1987, Stockholm, Anfang Publishers, Inc., Nordic Knitting. 1991, Loveland, CO, Interweave Press, pp 56-87.

9. Ringgard, Maj. *Silk Knitted Waistcoats: A 17th-century fashion item, in Fashionable Encounters: Perspectives and Trends in Textile and Dress in the Early Modern Nordic World*. Mathiassen, et all, eds., Oxford, UK, Oxbow Books, 2014, p. 95.

10. Ringgard, Maj. *Silk Knitted Waistcoats: A 17th-century fashion item in Fashionable Encounters: Perspectives and Trends in Textile and Dress in the Early Modern Nordic World*. Oxford, UK, Oxbow Books, 2014 ppp78-79.

11. Putman, Tyler Rudd, "Ran Away from the Subscriber" blog, October 2, 2010.

12. Falck, Erika Nordvall. *Fancy Mittens*. 2018, Jokkmokk, Ájtte, Svenskt fjäll—och samemseum, pp39-40.

13. These Victorian knitting Manuals all are accessible online fro the University of Southampton Library at: https://archive.org/details/victorianknittingmanuals\

14. Gottfridsson, Inger and Ingrid Gottfridsson, *The Mitten Book*. 1987, Asheville, NC, Lark Books, p 9. ***Note:*** This is a translation of *Gotlandska Stickmonster* published in 1981, that collected many of Hermanna's designs from hats, mittens and other garments, and used them to craft mitten patterns.

15. Overland, Viveka. *Bohus Stickning på nytt (The Revival)*. 2016, Udevalla, Bohusläns Museum, pp11–33.

16. Arvidsson, Harry. *Swedish Crafts and Craft Education, in Studies in Design Education Craft and Technology*, Vol. 21, no. 3, 1989 pps 157-161.

17. In her 1989 translation of Tvåändsstickat by Birgitta Dandanell and Ulla Danielsson, Robin Hansen sought to come up with a different translation for the term tvåändsstickning, feeling that the word itself didn't have an exact meaning and that it was too difficult for most English-speakers to pronounce. After experimenting with two-end, twisted, and various other forms, she settled on "twined," which has become synonymous with the technique. Unfortunately, this use is not correct as a textile technique. The act of twining is to wind, coil or wrap one thing around something else (rather than around itself)—in other words, two elements twisted around a third as in this diagram.

With the greatest respect to Ms. Hansen, I have chosen to retain the Swedish term or the literal translation of "two-end" for this technique throughout this book

Clear from many historic photos, knitters continued to hold their yarn with the right hand into the beginning of the 20th century.

18. Whitehouse, David. Woven Cloth dates back 27,000 years, BBC News, 14 June, 2000.

19. Greenfieldboyce, Nell. The Oldest String Ever Found May have been Made by Neanderthals, NPR Science, 10 April, 2020.

2 Design and Designers

There is a great deal of energy coming from the design community in Sweden. This work spans the field from traditional to very contemporary, and the yarns their designs feature are reasonably accessible internationally. A little bit of sleuthing through your local library and bookstore and a deep dive into the social media knitting site Ravelry can give you a good introduction to Swedish design and designers. Older publications tend to focus on mittens—knitted, felted and two-end knitting (*tvåändsstickning*). Current designers, however, while sometimes giving a nod to historic forms and patterns, add many interesting and innovative ideas to garments to give you endless inspiration.

If you are interested in purchasing Swedish yarns on your travels, why not consider knitting a garment by a Swedish designer? Whether your interests tend toward historical, traditional designs, or modern chic, you will easily find something to capture your imagination. I believe that the five designers profiled here represent not only a Swedish point of view, but also the international appeal of Nordic or Scandinavian-inspired design sensibility. Judge for yourself!

KARIN KAHNLUND

Karin Kahnlund is a master knitter, teacher, designer and well-known expert in the technique of *tvåändsstickning*. Perhaps the best description of her vast knowledge came from an advertisement I saw for one of her courses, which stated, "what Karin Kahnlund doesn't say about tvåändsstickning isn't worth hearing." After reading several books on the subject as well as taking one of her classes, I would have to agree. Her research on mittens, hats, socks and jackets in museum collections both in Dalarna Province and elsewhere, have allowed her to be able to identify the smallest differences from village to village both in design and technique, and to transmit that knowledge through her patterns and classes.

Many of Karin's patterns can be found in the book, *Tvåändstickat* by Brigitta Dandanell, Ulla Danielsson and Kersti Ankert (published by the Dalarnas Museum). While only available in Swedish, once you understand the methods and techniques of two-end knitting, it is possible to develop a feel for the designs and reproduce them without much translation. The pattern for "Center Blocks," a tvåändsstickning mitten pattern, is in the digital edition of the January/February 2011 *Piecework* Magazine available from Interweave Press.

A Antique mittens from Karin Kahnlund's collection.

SW photos

A *Gubbar och gummor by Karin Kahnlund*

Lars Dahlström, photographer

A Center Blocks Swedish Two-End Mittens *by Karin Kahnlund from the January/February 2011 issue of* PieceWork *magazine,* www.pieceworkmagazine.com.

Photo by Joe Coca, copyright Long Thread Media LLC

In 2011, Karin published a book of her own designs inspired by Jakob Kulle's 1892 *Svenska Mönster för Konstväfnader och Broderier* (Swedish Patterns for Art Weaves and Embroidery). These designs, provided in both Swedish and English, are completely contemporary, but with exquisite reference to traditional patterns and motifs.

The most thoroughly Swedish design can be found on the hat and mittens "Gubbar och gummor," (old men and women), stranded in navy blue, lime green and red on US size 0 (2mm) needles.

Her "Long Cardigan," knit side-to-side, features a lovely band of design down the back that is reminiscent of the band weaving found in traditional costume and household items. The shape of the garment is strikingly similar to the 16th century knitted waistcoats that can be found in museums in Sweden and Denmark (probably imported

⋏ *Long Cardigan by Karin Kahnlund*

Lars Dahlström, photographer

from Italy). Knit on 2.5mm needles (US 1.5), it is a serious undertaking, but a very straightforward project.

Karin's 2019 book on tvåändsstickning was published by Hemslöjdens Förlag. While only available in Swedish, it is lushly illustrated, and once you have mastered the techniques, it is straightforward to apply the mitten charts to your own work. In addition, the illustrations by Cecilia Ljungström of techniques such as braiding the cords at the cuff, are clear and easy to follow. It is a worthwhile addition to your knitting library and a good way to learn the craft.

ELSEBETH LAVOLD

Elsebeth Lavold is pretty much a household name for knitters around the world. In addition to knitting patterns, Elsebeth has lent her name to a series of yarns distributed by Knitting Fever, Inc. *Silky Wool* and *Hempathy* are two of the 20 varieties that are widely available. They have real versatility, great hand, and nice stitch definition. To give you an idea of its popularity, *Silky Wool* is represented in nearly 20,000 Ravelry projects….and

those are only the ones that have been documented on the site.

Elsebeth is of Norwegian heritage, was born in Denmark and has lived in Sweden for more than 50 years. She describes herself as Scandinavian, and enjoys a deep connection to the heritage of the area. With literally hundreds of designs to her credit, she is perhaps best known for her series *Viking Knits*. Work began on this collection in the 1990s. Elsebeth was inspired by the sinuous, interlaced curves found on archeological buckles, swords, carved stones—even a comb. While her first book (*Viking Patterns for Knitting*) focused on designs from Viking heritage, the second book (*Viking Knits & Ancient Ornaments*) includes interlaced designs that are found worldwide.

It might seem like a natural and direct jump from these designs to knitted cables, but the process was anything but simple. It's not just the crossing of one loop over another in cables that make the designs. There is a very complex application of increases and decreases in the knitting that both prevent the cable from distorting the knitted fabric, and that turn the cable in specific directions.

Anders Rydell, photographer

⌃ *Nigerian bronze bracelet (left); Vertical zigzag loops swatch (right)*

From Viking Knits & Ancient Ornaments, drawing by Elsabeth Lavold, photo by Anders Rydell

⌃ *Figure-8 and Ring Swatch, and Brooch from Gotland, Sweden. Viking Knits & Ancient Ornaments, p.60*

Drawing by Elsabeth Lavold, photo by Anders Rydell

Paired increases and decreases that slant in a specific direction are not new to knitting. But Elsebeth applied some very innovative methods to these stitches, both in the manner of working and in their location, to close off cables.

Her use of mitered corners in cables has been a groundbreaking innovation that many other designers have incorporated into their own projects, and have expanded the capability of many knitters to use cables in wholly new ways.

To see the range of ideas and develop an understanding of how translating those ideas and designs into knitting occured, *Viking Patterns for Knitting* is almost required reading. Once understood, knitting this type of cable is not difficult. But getting those curves and interlaced stitches from paper to yarn as part of the design process requires great skill, as well as much trial and error. It wasn't just a matter of figuring out the geometry and engineering of these stitches. She also needed to be able to explain them, and provide instructions to make them accessible to most knitters. She has accomplished that beautifully, with concise descriptions and excellent illustrations.

◁ *This sweater,* Signild, *with figure-8 cabled bands is pictured next to a rune stone. The designs from these stones helped inspire the series of sweater patterns for which Elsebeth became famous.* Signild *is from* Viking Knits and Ancient Ornaments, *Trafalgar Square Books, 2014*

Anders Rydell, photographer

With over 20 books and countless patterns to her credit, you might think that there aren't many ideas that could surprise you. However, her summery top "Mint" that turns into a shopping bag is yet another delightful innovation.

Elsebeth continues to find inspiration in historic artifacts and seems never at a loss for new ideas for her knitting. She also has reached the point where she designs more to please herself and knits things that she would like to wear rather than working toward material that is focused on the knitting market. In many respects, she has come full circle to where she started with the Viking patterns—a knitter/scholar who derives pleasure in doing something she hasn't done before just because she finds it interesting. It is this phenomenal creativity and precision, deeply rooted in over one thousand years of design tradition that she has made her own are, from my point of view, what defines Elsebeth Lavold.

KATARINA SEGERBRAND

Katarina Segerbrand completed her art training at the Academy of Design and Crafts, (Högskolan för design och konsthantverk and Textilhögskolan i Borås) and immediately went to work in the knitwear industry for the Coats Group and Marks & Kattens. She has enjoyed a long career as a designer for hand knitting, with numerous garments in American and European magazines, like *Vogue*, the Norwegian magazine *Familian Strikk*, and *Stikat & Sånt* and *Allers mm* in Sweden.

Katarina has a real knack for stranded color work that has a completely original look even when she uses traditional patterns. However, her execution of stylized

⋏ MInt *top and shopping bag, designed by Elsebeth Lavold*
Anders Rydell, photographer

⋏ *Stylized floral pullovers by Katarina Sergerbrand*

Ull Alderin photos (left and right), Vogue Magazine *(center)*

Jack Deutsch for Vogue Knitting

floral designs like the one from 2017 (above left), are unique. Her interpretation of this traditional form is very contemporary and fresh, and gives the garments a visual lightness that is very striking and recognizable as her own style (the pattern for this sweater can be found on page 123).

Check out the fall 2018 issue of *Vogue Knitting* magazine for her Fair Isle pullover knit in Blue Sky Fibers' Woolstok Worsted (center). The garment on the right (above) was designed for an exhibition inspired by the Swedish artist Karin Larsson. The pattern can be found on Ravelry.

If you visit her blog or Ravelry page, you'll see dozens of free patterns that can be found on the Järbo yarn website. Järbo yarns are available throughout Scandinavia, as well as shops in Germany, Iceland and the Netherlands. They also are sized according to Craft Council designations (e.g., Gästrike 1 ply is a size 1, or fingering weight wool, and Gästrike 3-ply is in yarn group 4, or worsted weight). This makes it easier to substitute your own yarns if what she originally used isn't immediately available.

It's not just color work that distinguishes Katarina's design style. Her lacework is equally exciting. The summer 2019 *Vogue Knitting* issue captures the clean lines and visual simplicity of her design ethos. It features a deep band of lace and a fringe finish on a short summer dress worked in cotton.

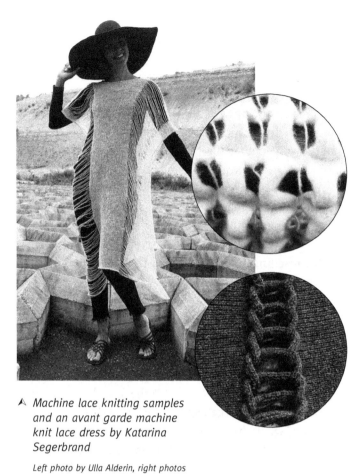

Katarina has recently been experimenting with lace/short rows for machine knitting—a return to her early designing for industry. This work is particularly innovative and fun, and her creative combinations of knitting and felting (photo left) will make you want to dust off your knitting machine. Part of her motivation for this new direction is teaching machine knitting to students at the Swedish School of Textiles at the University of Borås. The School is housed in the Textile Fashion Center, together with the Swedish Textile Museum and the Fashion Gallery—home to fashion entrepreneurial start-ups. The synergy between Katarina's crossover design using traditional plus avant-garde makes her the perfect teacher for these fledgling designers.

She is shown below (left) at her knitting machine, along with three garments that capture both the versatility of lace/short rows and how they ironically become a foundation for avant-garde accents.

⋏ *Machine lace knitting samples and an avant garde machine knit lace dress by Katarina Segerbrand*

Left photo by Ulla Alderin, right photos by Katarina Segerbrand

IVAR ASPLUND

I ended up meeting quite a few people in Sweden almost by accident. I was given the names of several designers by the *Sticka!* Organization. In one instance, the person I contacted wasn't going to be in the country when I was in Stockholm, but she gave me the name of another designer she said I absolutely needed to meet — Ivar Asplund.

⋏ *Ivar is wearing a sweater of his own design worked in two-end knitting technique (tvåändsstickning)*

Johanne Ländin, photographer

⋏ *Ivar Asplund's contemporary adaptations of a traditional tvåändsstickning mittens*

SW photo

⋏ *Katarina Segerbrand in her studio*

SW photo

He was described as a really interesting individual and designer, and that was certainly an understatement. His recent book of knitting patterns *Sticka Flätor* features scarves, hats, shawls and sweaters that showcase gorgeous cables and textures, but what I really appreciate about his designs are the relaxed and comfortable lines of his garments. Each of his sweaters immediately looks like it is about to be your next favorite "live in" garment, and while the patterns are anything but ordinary they are not difficult to knit. And good news for those of you who don't read Swedish (including me), the book was published in English in the fall of 2019.

Ivar's book reminds me of some of the cookbooks I've bought just because they were so beautiful and were

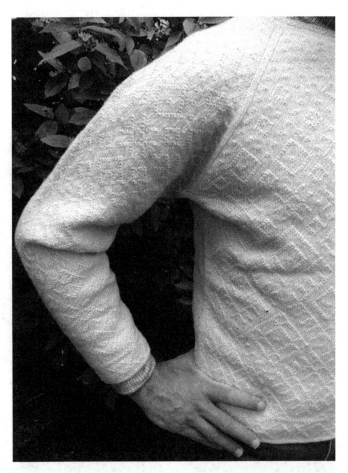

∧ *The sweater he is wearing here is a very special example of the tvåändsstickning technique that would be nearly impossible to turn into a commercial pattern. If you look closely, while the raised patterns have similarities, they do not repeat vertically. Beyond that, this sweater tells an eloquent story of its maker. It has the elegance and perfection that Ivar brings to all of his designs. It blends art, craft, and a deep understanding of the mechanics of knitting that are all of the hallmarks of a master.*

Johanne Ländin, photographer

bound to give me inspiration. I find myself sitting down and savoring the pages one-by-one without any particular plan to pick up my needles. It's a lush publication, with wonderful photographs, meticulous illustrations and precise drawings of his cable construction techniques. In my opinion, it will be a classic that you'll want not only on your shelf for reference, but will turn to again and again for its well-crafted patterns.

As a child, Ivar learned to knit when his grandmother began to teach his sister. He asked to be taught as well, and in the end, it was he, rather than his sister, who became a knitter. He credits his grandmother not only for the teaching, but her guidance that pushed him to explore and grow as a knitter.

While patterns in two-end knitting do not appear in *Sticka Flätor*, they were the examples he brought to show me when we met. His designs draw strongly on historic examples, and are beautifully made.

In addition to knitting and design, Ivar also works at a local yarn store—Litet Nystan (in the Stockholm neighborhood of Mariatorget, and a quick walk from the subway stop) where he also teaches classes. You'll also find him as a regular instructor at Handarbetets Vänner — a school of advanced textile craft, as well as craft festivals and knitting venues around Sweden.

As a teacher, Ivar is very interested in giving his students a strong grounding in knitting technique. Once a beginning knitter understands and internalizes the basics, they are off and running on their own adventure. The fact that they also get to make something beautiful, warm, and from their own hands is all added benefit.

KRISTIN BLOM

Kristin Blom is a knitter and relatively new knitwear designer from Uppsala who is nearly impossible to categorize. You can find her designs in *The Knitter* and *Pom Pom Quarterly* as well as on Ravelry. With an allergy to the lanolin in wool, the garments she knits for herself are interesting combinations of fibers like cotton and kapok, or alpaca and silk.

Inside the box (next page) is a design that speaks to Kristin's interest in designing outside the box by focusing on the backside of garments. She refers to these as the "va va va voom" view, and in addition to these eye-catching elements, she constructs these tops with elegant necklines and simple, but never boring textures.

With a youngster of her own, it isn't surprising that Kristin has designed a number of sweaters for children. *Elliott's Jumper* has multiple options for the knitter's own interpretations, and *Karussel* even has an infant version without the carousel animals.

Kristin's color work uses the "invisible stranding" technique popularized by the TECHknitter Blog. This technique is particularly useful for working with yarns that are highly contrasting (such as the red and white in *Karussel* below), or where yarns are worked in a slightly loose gauge. This technique has the added value of preventing little fingers from being caught in the floats.

A graphic designer by day and knitter by night, Kristin began seriously working on marketing her own designs while working with British designer Anna Maltz on her book, *Penguin: a Knit Collection*. Anna encouraged Kristin to include *Aptendoytes*, an interestingly shaped cardigan with crossover fronts.

In looking through her designs, you may find it difficult to put your finger on Kristin's style. But that's almost the point. As a designer she is constantly evolving and changing, experimenting and playing. There is a joy and energy to her style that matches her personality.

⋏ Inside the Box

Johan Wahlgren, photographer

⋏ *Elliott's Jumper*

Kristin Blom, photographer

⋏ *Karusel*

Madelene Linderstam, photographer

⋏ *Aptendoytes*

Photo by Elle Benton for Anna Maltz

3 Swedish Fleece and Fibers

SWEDISH SHEEP

There are at least 19 breeds of sheep in Sweden, one as old as the Viking Civilization (8th–11th centuries) and still located on Gotland Island, an ancient Viking trading port. These sheep—the *Gutefår*—are few in number these days, but like several other breeds are part of a conservation program to preserve unique animals and other local breeds.

Most of the distinctive Swedish sheep are known as *landrace* animals. This means that through isolation and traditional agricultural breeding methods, these sheep have developed their specific characteristics over time and have adapted to their local natural environment.

Early interbreeding of the Northern European short tail breeds formed the base for the Swedish sheep gene pool, and are descendants of *Mouflon*, the oldest domesticated sheep originating in Asia Minor.

Interbreeding has continued throughout history. Some of the most iconic sheep in Sweden—such as *Gotlandsfår*—are a product of the 20th century, with the ancient Swedish *Gute* having been bred with *Karakuls* and *Romanovs* to eliminate the horns, and improve both the fleece and meat quality.

▲ *Mouflon Sheep*
Wikimedia commons, Volker.G

▲ Jämtland *sheep*
Courtesy of Yarns & Barns, UllForum Spinneri, photographer

The most recent breed to develop from purposeful crossbreeding is the *Jämtlandsfår*, a cross that includes *Svea* (a mix of *Finull* and *Texel*) and *Merino*. Jämtland sheep were designated as an official breed in 2011. These sheep were bred specifically as competition for imported merino to offer a local, sustainable wool.

Nils Dahlbeck (1911–1998), a Swedish botanist and radio/television personality, is widely credited for his work in the early 1990s to identify the native sheep breeds he remembered from his childhood. At that point, most of those breeds were near extinction, due in large part to the decline in value of these animals. Then as now, sheep were used primarily for food, and about ¾ of the wool was burned or thrown away for lack of a market. This is changing, and with news coverage about discarded wool and a strong community of shepherds and crafters pushing for local and sustainable products, there is a growing demand for local wool and the conservation of endangered breeds.

The largest group interested in the preservation of traditional Swedish breeds (Föreningen Svenska Allmogefår) maintains a gene bank and recognizes 10 unique types. In addition, the Swedish Sheep Breeders Association (Svenska Fåravelsförbundet), established in 1917, promotes commercial production of both meat and wool. Two smaller organizations have developed over the past few years to provide a mechanism for small-scale producers to make contact with individuals interested in purchasing wool. One, *Swedish Fibre* (owned by Sandy Zeterlund), works through the Etsy website to provide locally sourced fiber, fleece and yarn to an international clientele. The website is a very good place to begin to learn about Swedish breeds. The other, *Ullförmedlingen*, (developed by Fia Söderberg), maintains a Facebook site and Wool Agency website that allows producers to list their products. Potential buyers are able to purchase directly from the farmers and shepherds. Both enterprises are small, but growing, and opportunities for sale outside of Sweden are dependent on the seasonal availability of products, and the willingness of individuals to work with international buyers.

Reading about Swedish sheep can be a little confusing, because some of the words that describe wool characteristics also are the names of individual breeds. Within this book we have attempted to differentiate between wool types and wool breeds by capitalizing and italicizing the word when we are naming the sheep breed. Several wool types can be found within a single fleece, and this is particularly true of the conservation breeds that can be very heterogeneous. Following are some useful descriptors:

Finull is wool with lots of crimp and is mostly or only undercoat. The *Finull* breed is this type, but parts of the fleece of *Värmland* and *Dalapäls* wool can be finull type, with fine, soft fiber.

Rya wool is both undercoat and outercoat known for its sturdy texture. *Klövsjö* is usually a rya type, as are parts of the fleece of *Dalapäls*, *Värmland*, and *Rya*.

Gobelängull and pälsull are synonyms for fleece that is mostly outercoat. *Gotland* and *Swedish Leicester* sheep are this type. *Gotland* sheep are also sometimes referred to as pälsfår, or "pelt sheep."

Vadmalsull is a wool type with lots of undercoat and just a few strands of outercoat, and features a triangular shaped staple. The name relates to the excellent fulling characteristics of the wool (Vadmal is a woven and heavily fulled fabric). Parts of *Dalapäls* and *Värmland* fleece can be this type.

Our purpose of spinning and knitting from the fleece of individual breeds is to give an idea of the characteristics of the breed and identify those qualities that hand spinners and knitters might desire to work with. In the commercial market, most yarns are a mix of different types of fiber. *Jämtland* and *Finull* are both very soft for

⋎ Staple types from the left: Rya, pälsul, vadmal and finul staples. All are from the same Värmland fleece.

JW photo

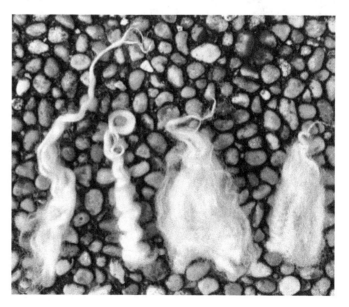

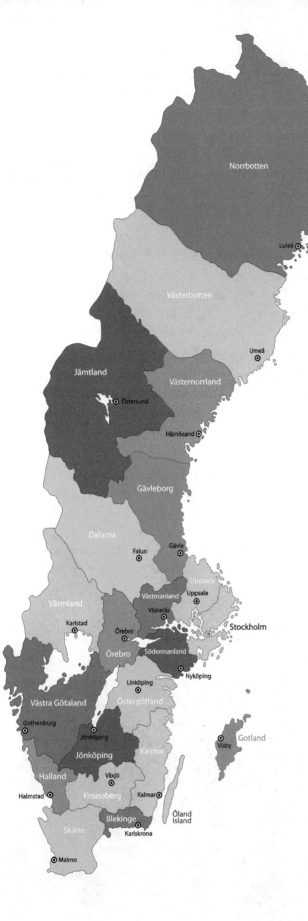

hand knitting, and may be found on their own. However, the very popular *Gotland* is slippery and difficult to spin. Consequently, many mills include 20-25% of imported *Merino*, or *Finull* and other local fibers to create their yarns.

There also was test spinning and knitting from commercial mill products. Some of those are included in this chapter, but most of the mixed fleece and yarns are reviewed in the chapter on Spinning Mills or in Josefin's spinning notes.

Fleece to test spin and knit were not universally available during the writing of this book. We have tried to list all of the known breeds and their attributes in hopes of continuing to study them in the future. There will be ongoing information about Swedish sheep and wool on our blogs, as well as real-time updates about availability as we find new information.

You can find us at:
Josefin: *https://waltin.se/josefinwaltinspinner/*
Sara: *https://aknitwizard.com/*

Åsenfår

Most *Åsen* sheep can be found near the village of Åsen in Dalarna Province. They are members of the group known as forest sheep—a hardy breed able to live on limited

Courtesy of Mikael Suvanto

⅄ Åsen *locks are airy with lots of undercoat and just a few strands of outercoat*

JW photo

⅄ Åsen *sheep at Skansen Outdoor Museum in Stockholm*

SW photo

pasture in the summer and poor feed during the winter. They are sometimes used to keep the landscape clear, even eating the bark of trees if they run out of options. *Åsen* are small in size, and the rams are typically horned. The fleece is double coated, but there may be little difference between the outer and inner coats in some of the fleece. The wool itself is smooth, with nice curls and waves, and ranges from glossy rya to finull in texture.

Lambs are usually born black with white and/or brown spots. As they age, the colors vary greatly within the flock, ranging from black and grey to white. Crafters find the wool good for both spinning and felting.

Josefin's Thoughts on Spinning

As the *Åsen* wool that I have spun was very open and airy it was a delight to process and spin. It was mostly white with some grey fibers; lots of undercoat and just a few strands of outercoat in typical vadmal staples (see description of staple types above).

⋀ *2-ply low-twist yarn spun from the rolags (left) and hand-carded rolags of Åsen wool (right)*

JW photos

The outercoat was around 10 cm and the undercoat around 8 cm. I wanted to keep the airiness and decided to card and spin a woolen yarn. The soft undercoat gave lots of air to the rolags and the strong outercoat kept the fibers together and the rolag in a defined shape. The characteristics I wanted to emphasize were the airiness, the lightness, and the straightforwardness of the staples. I had an image in my head of a very light, perhaps slightly rough, yarn similar to an Icelandic-style yarn. My ideas worked out the way I had planned. I spun the rolags with English longdraw into a light yarn with a low twist. The airiness gave a roundedness and halo to the finished yarn.

In my view *Åsen* wool is an all-around wool that can be prepared and spun in many ways for a wide range of projects and textile techniques. I just chose one.

The second fleece I bought and haven't spun yet has white and very soft undercoat and black outercoat in a very dramatic look. It has long staples and I am thinking of spinning this one worsted for a weaving yarn.

Sara's Thoughts on Knitting

I have to agree with Josefin that *Åsen* fleece produces a good all-around yarn that has the potential for multiple uses and that the halo she was able to achieve with the low twist is really pretty. I can see it as the yoke for a raglan sweater where the wool was used as the accent rather than then background/main color, as the subtle mix of shades of light grey and white give added

⋀ *Swatch knit from Josefin's handspun Åsen yarn*

SW photo

depth and texture to a design. That being said, I didin't find it appealing as a yarn to go next to the skin. The halo comes from the fibers of the outercoat that protrude from the yarn and are really scratchy. I was surprised at that because the yarn felt much more smooth as I was handling it during knitting. I'm actually thinking that it would be really interesting to mix this with something like angora to add some real textural interest to the angora and really soften up the *Åsen*. I think this is a fiber worth investigating further.

Dalapälsfår

Another of the landrace sheep originating from Dalarna Province, the name of the *Dalapäls* sheep references its use in addition to its origin ("Dala" for Dalarna Province and päls for its use as a "fur" or "pelt"). The traditional

JW photo

jacket from this region, called *kasung* was made of sheepskin, and the edgings of white wool locks resemble those of the *Dalapäls* sheep.

△ *Photos from 19th century Sweden showing* kasung *jackets*

Photographer unknown (left). Courtesy of the Nordiska museet (NM.0038500), Karl Lärka, photographer (top)

The *Dalapäls* sheep are quite small, around 30 kg for ewes and 50 kg for rams. They have a strong sense for the flock and are very suspicious of strangers. This may come from the fact that they have traditionally grazed in the woods and have developed an alertness for enemies like wolf and bear. The wool is usually white, although some have grey spots. Lambs may be born black, but turn grey or white as they grow.

Josefin's Thoughts on Spinning

Dalapäls wool is a double-coated wool with strong and shiny outer coat and fine, soft and warm under coat. The most common fiber type is the long and wavy staple. This wool type has little or no crimp.

Shorter, wavy and even crimpy staples do occur and the fleece is not even across the body of the sheep. This gives a spinner many choices in spinning the wool. A shepherd or shepherdess can have a small flock of sheep and still get lots of different wool types.

Three characteristics of the *Dalapäls* wool are shine, fineness and versatility. It also is very easy to spin. Even though the outercoat is long and strong it is still very fine and can be spun into a next-to-skin yarn. The undercoat is of course even finer than the outer coat. The locks are very lofty at the base and the undercoat is soft and silky.

Because of the variation of the wool between individuals and over the body of one individual sheep, *Dalapäls* wool is very versatile. It is possible to find anything from from 25 cm long silky and wavy locks to 5 cm curly or even crimpy staples. If you sort the fleece according to wool characteristics and also separate the fiber types you could get a wide variety of yarns—particularly if you are a hand spinner.

Combing the outer coat for a worsted yarn and carding the under coat for a woolen yarn are good choices. You can just as well card or comb the fiber types together.

Picking out the longest locks and separating the undercoat from the outercoat can give you two beautiful yarns—a strong and shiny worsted yarn and a soft

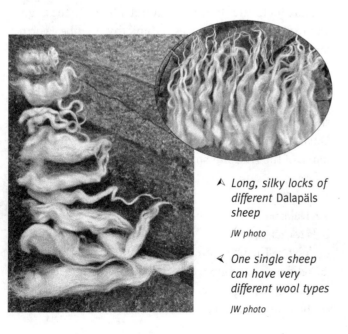

△ *Long, silky locks of different* Dalapäls *sheep*

JW photo

◁ *One single sheep can have very different wool types*

JW photo

△ Dalapäls *wool can be spun in many different ways. Left to right: Carded undercoat, woolen spun on a spinning wheel. Combed outercoat, worsted spun on a spinning wheel. Undercoat and outercoat teased and carded together, woolen spun on a spinning wheel. Flick-carded locks, spun worsted on a supported spindle from the cut end*

JW photo

and warm woolen yarn. I would use double row combs to separate the fiber types and pull the outercoat off. Perhaps I would even comb a second time to separate more and spin worsted from the lovely tops. The leftovers in the combs are the soft and airy undercoat that I would card into rolags and and spin woolen. This way you will get two very different yarns with different characteristics. You can see the difference in the image previous page, the first from the left is the carded undercoat and the second is the combed outercoat.

Another way to create a beautiful *Dalapäls* yarn is to card or comb the locks as they are without separating the fiber types. I would do this with the medium and shorter length staples. Carding and spinning woolen would give you a soft yarn that still has some strength and shine. If I were to comb the locks I would use single row combs that won't separate the fiber types as much as the double row combs. Spinning the combed top worsted would result in a strong and shiny yarn that would still have some softness.

In another *Dalapäls* yarn I spun I wanted to keep the fiber types together. The locks in this yarn are the very longest locks that the shepherdess has picked out from several fleeces. I have flick carded each lock individually and spun the locks from the cut end. This way I will get both outer coat and under coat in the yarn.

The z-plied yarn was spun on a supported spindle, my preference for spinning flick-carded locks. The slowness of the technique allows me to watch the process and focus on quality. Spinning from the lock can be a challenge since the fibers don't get as much of a separation

⌃ Staple, flick carded staple and supported spindle with Dalapäls *wool (left), and finished yarn (right)*
JW photos

compared to a hand-combed top. The yarn I get from spinning from the cut end of flick carded locks is strong, shiny and still soft. When I spin it on a supported spindle I also get the quality and the evenness I want.

Sara's Thoughts on Knitting

Josefin gifted me a small ball of her z-spun *Dalapäls* yarn, and it was so lovely that I had to put it aside quite a while before diving in. I had seen her sleeves (below) and knew that this yarn was anything but "usual." One of the remarkable things about working with materials that are made by hand is that they often radiate the pure joy coming from their maker. I decided that this small amount

◅ Spinning counter-clockwise to get a z-plied yarn for twined knitting

Dan Waltin, photographer

◅ Josefin's knitting project with handspun Dalapäls, a pair of sleeves in two-end or tvåändsstickning

JW photo

of yarn needed to be rationed to allow it to become the top edge of a pair of mittens that could stand out from the rest of the design. I also wanted to use every inch, so quite a bit of planning went into this test knit so that both pieces would be the same size and have equal design features.

In the end, I decided to do a very small swatch and work from where I had stopped with the Wålstedts Ullspinneri z-ply for comparison. This was one of those choices that had a really interesting outcome. For a start, there is no way to compare Josefin's hand spun to Wålstedts z-ply for any number of reasons. First and foremost, they aren't the same fibers, and that turned out to be the apples to oranges comparison. The *Dalapäls* yarn is as Josefin had hoped, strong and shiny. It is also quite soft, and even with the density of tvåändsstickning will be reasonable to wear against the skin. By comparison, the Wålstedts yarn is extremely tight in the spin and more rustic, but it has an almost slippery feel (due to the inclusion of *Rya*). I ended up only working two rows with the *Dalapäls* because I felt like I had a good feel for the fiber very quickly, and plan to rip back to save the yarn for better use. This is a breed I can easily see returning to again and again. It does work well, spun S and plied Z, but now I really want to try some z-spun s-plied yarn to see how differently it feels. As with so many of the Swedish sheep, we are only seeing the very tip of the iceberg of possibilities.

Finullsfår

In their blog, the company A New Sweden notes that the *Finull* sheep are an old relative of merino sheep that were in Sweden as early as the 18th century. Like other merino-type yarns, fiber from *Finull* is certainly valued for its soft, creamy texture, and comfort of wearing next to the skin.

∧ *Finull sheep*
Dan Waltin, photographer

The fleece of *Finull* can be white, brown, black, and sometimes speckled. It is either crimpy or wavy, and with a staple of between 15 and 25 microns, falls into the category of a fine or medium wool that is good for both knitting and felting.

While these sheep are not part of the heritage gene bank, they usually are listed as a conservation breed. They probably are not in danger of extinction, and are an important component of many of the yarns produced in Sweden, often used to modify the hand of the more robust, hard fibers of some of the other native types.

Josefin's Thoughts on Spinning

The first fleece I ever dug my inexperienced hands into back in 2012 was the fleece from Pia-Lotta the *Finull* lamb. For this reason *Finull* is my home base wool. It is the kind of wool I know the best and feel confident with. It is one of the three Swedish breeds bred for the fleece as it is very soft and fine-fibered. The main characteristics of *Finull* that I want to show are the softness, the shine and the crimp. I usually spin finull woolen from hand-carded rolags. Before that I always tease the locks. This might

∧ *A sweater knit in handspun 3-ply woolen* Finull *yarn. Stripes in* Jämtland *wool*

Dan Waltin, photographer

∧ *Tvåändsstickning swatch worked in Wålstedts z-ply (orange) and Josefin's handspun* Dalapäls

SW photo

sound tedious, and it is. But the process is truly worth the effort as it eliminates most nepps and short bits. Since the fibers are so fine, there is a risk of the tips breaking in the carding process. If I tease the staples with a flick card before carding, the broken tips end up in the flick card instead of in the rolag and the finished yarn.

Even though *Finull* is a mainly soft yarn with basically only undercoat (or at least it is difficult to tell undercoat and outercoat apart) it still has a subtle shine. I spin it 2- or 3-plied and usually quite fine. Because of the fine crimp the yarn is quite elastic and keeps the shape of the garment. *Finull* makes a perfect yarn for next to skin garments.

Sara's Thoughts on Knitting

If I were confined to using only one yarn, I might opt for *Finull*. It is a very fine fiber that is extremely soft, and it can be used for anything from baby clothes to outerwear, depending on how it is spun and plied.

The brown swatch is from Swedish Fibre. The cables stand out well, and the purl and knit stitches have crisp definition. This particular yarn is a 12 wpi (sport weight) 2-ply. The singles have been fairly loosely plied, giving the yarn a very rounded, lofty feel.

Josefin's denim blue handspun also has a lofty profile. At 14 wpi, her 3-ply yarn is compactly spun but very round. Like the commercial spun, this yarn has excellent stitch definition, lovely drape and a very soft hand.

Because of its versatility and softness, *Finull* is frequently blended with other wools to improve their performance. *Finull* on its own can be found at Solkunstens Spinnverkstad. Blended, *Finull* can be found at most spinning mills, and some, like Filtmakeriet use it in most of their yarns. It also is frequently a component of the Höner och Eir *Nutiden* Yarn

Finull sheep also are often crossed with other breeds to bring out specific characteristics of wool or meat. One example of a *Finull* cross with *Gotland* produced a wool that is both different from the individual breed fleece, and different than any of the fleece mixes coming from the spinning mills.

One of Josefin's early spinning efforts came came from a lamb called Sounnie who was a 75/25 cross of *Gotland* and *Finull*. The yarn coming from Sounnie's fleece feels much more like that of a *Gotland* lamb than a purposely blended yarn. That being said, this is a lovely yarn that can be worn next to the skin because it was spun and plied softly. Had this yarn been given a tight twist, it wouldn't have felt that good in a garment. The other advantage of the method Josefin used in handling the fleece really accentuates the glossy character of the wool. Josefin is fond of saying that the benefit of hand spinning is the ability of the spinner to bring out the superpowers hidden within the wool. This is a great example of that idea.

Fjällnäsfår

The *Fjällnäs* is a recent addition to the Swedish Gene Bank. Once common in the north, the breed was "rediscovered" in the village of Fjällnäs, Lappland (Norrbotten

ᐱ A swatch knit of Josefin's handspun from fleece of the crossbred lamb, Sounnie

ᐱ Two examples of Fjällnäs sheep

Courtesy of Mikael Ågren

Province), in the beginning of the 21st century. Gunhild Stålnacke and her husband received a few of these sheep as a wedding gift in 1952. The sheep were a type common in the area known for their short tails.

Fjällnäs are good at managing themselves in the spring and summer when they are left in the mountain forests to forage. Traditionally they were collected together in the fall after the hay was harvested.

The double-coated fleece is usually white with a yellow tone; some have a coloring similar to deer. Compared to other breeds with the same type of fleece, *Fjällnäs* have a much larger proportion of undercoat as a result of their living in very cold conditions. Their wool has been used for everyday mittens, socks, sweaters and long underwear for protection against the harsh winter by the reindeer herders. The sheepskins were also used to shove into the foot of sleeping bags used by the Sami.

This breed is critically endangered, and there are very few of these sheep in Sweden (only 40 breeding ewes in 2012). They are not yet a commercially viable type for fleece and yarn.

Gestrikefår

Gestrike sheep originate from the village of Mörtebo in Gästrikland in the east of Sweden. The color of the *Gestrike* sheep varies greatly and they are often variegated or spotted. Some lambs are born black, others brownish or white and sometimes pale in color with increasing age.

These sheep are double-coated. The wool is quite varied but predominantly tapestry wool or rya type wool, with long wavy outercoat and dense undercoat. This is an endangered species,

although there has been recent interest in increasing flocks. The result is that the fleece can now sometimes be found from individual farmers.

The *Gestrike* wool Josefin obtained came from three ewes who live at the Vallby open-air museum. The wool is of mostly rya and fur type but some staples are of vadmal and finull type. The outercoat is long and very shiny and the undercoat is fine and soft. Kemp fibers add a rustic feeling to the wool and keep the staples light and open. The openness makes the staples easy to process. The longest outercoat fibers are over 15 cm and the undercoat is around 8–10 cm.

Josefin's thoughts on Spinning

In a yarn I want to emphasize the lightness, the shine and the rusticity. My initial desire is to separate the wool and use the strong and shiny outercoat for warp and the softer undercoat for weft. But since this book is focused mainly on knitting I decided to card the wool in its entirety and spin a woolen knitting yarn.

I teased the wool staple by staple with a flick card and carded rolags. Some would think it adventurous to card such long wool. It would be had all the wool been over 15 cm—the fibers would be doubled in the rolags and make a tangled mess. In this case, though, there is a mix of long

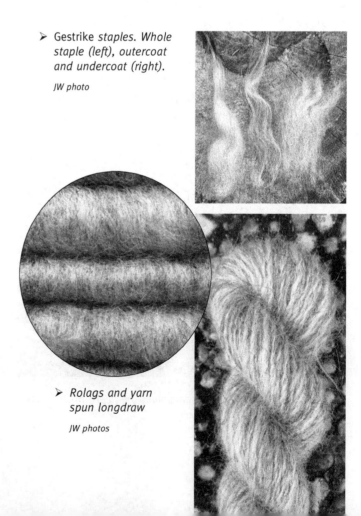

➤ Gestrike *staples. Whole staple (left), outercoat and undercoat (right).*

JW photo

➤ *Rolags and yarn spun longdraw*

JW photos

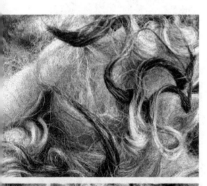

➢ *Raw Gestrike fleece (top) and washed fleece (bottom)*

JW photos

A Gestrike *ram*

Courtesy of Erica Andersson

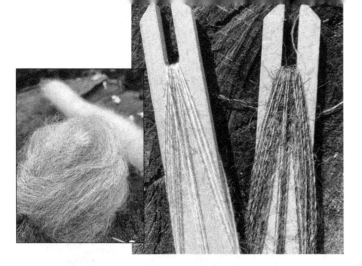

⅄ Processed outercoat and undercoat (left)
Yarns spun for warp and weft (right)

JW photos

⅄ Swatch from Josefin's Gestrike handspun yarn

SW photo

and medium fibers. The undercoat builds the foundation of the rolags while the long outercoat binds them together. The yarn will be airy and strong. The undercoat will give the yarn softness and the outercoat will bring the shine.

I spun the yarn with longdraw and a low twist and 2-plied. Spinning this *Gestrike* wool required a lot of attention. The combination of the airiness and the shiny fibers made the yarn pull apart several times but after a while I found a method that worked well. I didn't support the yarn with my front hand as I usually do with longdraw. With only my back (fiber) hand on the yarn the fibers could communicate with me and the back hand knew what to do. The yarn didn't pull apart anymore and I got a better spinning flow. An open and slippery wool like this also requires firm and tight rolags.

With a different fleece I was able to go back to my original idea of spinning for a woven textile with the outercoat and undercoat separated and processed.

Sara's thoughts on Knitting

Gestrike does have lovely sheen, but I don't think that it's very successful as a knitting wool on its own. It is quite rustic in feel and even spun to accentuate all of its good qualities, the fiber has a hard, springy texture that isn't enjoyable to work with. I think Josefin's idea of using this as a weaving yarn with separately processed outercoat and undercoat is a really interesting idea. I'm looking forward to seeing what she can accomplish. It also would be fun to see how each of these samples (warp and weft) work with other breed samples to see if the *Gestrike* can lend its good qualities to another yarn with its own unique qualities.

Gotlandsfår

Gotland sheep are probably the best known of the Swedish breeds and the most prevalent. Developed in the 1920s and 30s, they are a crossbreed of *Romanov* (from Russia) and *Karakuls* (from Central Asia) with the native *Gutefår*. These sheep have spread into Great Britain, Denmark and the Netherlands, and now can be found in the US and New Zealand.[1] Although they are a Swedish breed, they are not endangered and so are not part of the conservation program.

⅄ Gotland *ewe at Öströö Fårfarm.*

SW photos

Gotlands are a multipurpose breed, being grown for their wool, their pelts and their fleece. The cross breeding has eliminated the horns, and the improved fleece is more uniform in composition than the more rustic *Gute*. Their fleece is long and lustrous and can be found in shades of grey from silver to nearly black. The adult fleece is fairly rustic in hand, but the lambs-wool is quite fine and reasonably soft.

Josefin's Thoughts on Spinning

Newly shorn *Gotlands* is very shiny, with a uniform staple length. The fleece is

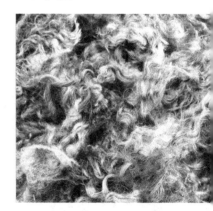

⅄ Gotland *lamb fleece*

JW photo

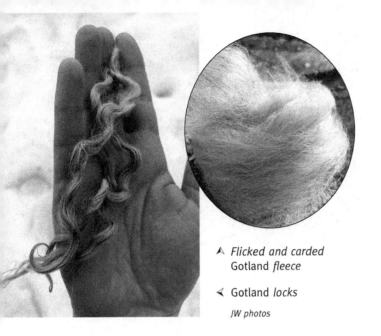

⋏ Flicked and carded Gotland *fleece*

⋖ Gotland *locks*

JW photos

⋏ *Josefin's knitting project from handspun Gotland 2-ply*

Don Waltin, photographer

mostly outercoat and very little undercoat, giving it more of a wave than crimp. The staples are quite long and very dense, and the fibers very slippery (making it a challenge to spin). Because of the risk of the fibers falling apart, some spinning mills have difficulty spinning pure *Gotland*, and often blend it with up to 25% of a finull type.

If *Gotland* fleece is allowed to sit, it may become compacted (almost felted) and will require intensive processing to prepare it for spinning. Because of its density, carding combs can only be loaded with a few flicked locks without taking tremendous strength to card.

Because of its density, *Gotland* wool also has lots of drape. To keep it from becoming too heavy, I spun the hand-combed top with a short forward draw and low twist on my wheel. The result was a 2-ply fingering yarn

with both shine and drape. The significant preparation time also resulted in significant waste (50-55%), but a very consistent yarn.

Sara's Thoughts on Knitting

Commercial *Gotland* yarn was my introduction to Swedish wool. While it completely enchanted me with the range of natural colors, I failed to note that the most prevalent brand (Yilet) was a mix of Swedish *Gotland* and Falkland Islands *Merino*, spun in Denmark. I had hoped for a 100% Swedish yarn (yarn from Swedish breeds), but was still sufficiently captivated by the rustic feel of the yarn with its significant halo to immediately want to cast on for a sweater.

I've had the opportunity to work with many of the *Gotland* yarns spun in Sweden, and each company seems

⋎ *Tailspun yarn from* Gotland *neck locks*

JW photo

⋎ *Handspun* Gotland *2-ply*

JW photo

⋎ *The top and middle swatches are from Yllet yarn (2-ply sport weight). The bottom swatch is from Öströö Fårfarm; a 3-ply sport weight 100% Gotland yarn*

SW photo

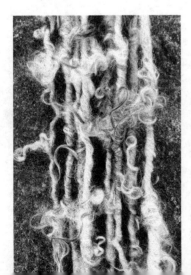

to be able to produce a unique type of yarn. For example, the Öströö yarn is very tightly plied and produces a very robust and durable fabric. The Yllet yarn produced decent stitch definition in the swatch (previous page), but across a larger part of a sweater I was knitting, the stitches began to look "muddy" because the yarn produces a significant halo.

This sweater above (named for the Samuel Beckett play *Waiting for Godot*; a reference to the fact that the recipient had to wait a very long time to wear it, and it seemed, at times, like it might never be finished) had two challenges: 1) the yarn is scratchy next to the skin because the "halo" is produced by outercoat fibers that have popped out of the twist. The garment needed to be designed to be worn over another garment, and 2) I needed to use a stitch pattern for the two-color areas that had enough depth to effectively differentiate the two colors. This actually became the most important part of the design feature—necessitated by the fact that I wasn't able to acquire enough of either color when I bought it to make the entire sweater alone.

Since *Gotland* wool is found in a variety of commercial yarns in Sweden and the US, and also can be purchased from craft fairs and wool festivals as fleece, roving, or sometimes handspun yarns, the variety is a little daunting. There is a huge difference between the wool from adult sheep and lambs, and between commercial yarns that use the whole fleece versus handspun yarns that have been processed to remove coarse fibers. I would say that any time spent on processing the fleece is worth the effort if you are spinning your own wool, and even the coarsest of the commercial yarns is so shiny and beautiful that you will have trouble keeping it out of your stash.

There are more reviews of *Gotland* wool in chapter 5.

Gutefår

Gute sheep are the most primitive and likely the oldest breed in Sweden. One of the landrace animals, it is native to the island of Gotland. The breed is one of the Northern European short-tailed sheep group, the oldest of which is believed to be Old Norwegian. *Gute* is an abbreviation for Gotland outdoor sheep

⋀ Gute *ewe*

JW photo

(Gotländskt utegångsfår), and it also refers to a person that has lived in Gotland for at least three generations. These sheep are a conservation breed, and there is some disagreement as to what constitutes a pure bred *Gute*. Some can be found on Gotland Island and some of their descendants can be seen at the Skansen Outdoor Museum in Stockholm.

Gute wool has a variety of qualities, from very fine undercoat to black kemp. There is considerable variation between individuals and also over the body of one individual. This made *Gute* sheep ideal for a small household. Go back a hundred years and see yourself as a small farmer with lots of different kinds of wool for lots of purposes from only a small flock of *Gute* sheep.

Gute wool has a long outercoat of around 40 microns, a very fine undercoat of around 17 microns, and kemp. All these fiber types are present all over the fleece, but to varying degrees. The long and strong outercoat protects the sheep from wind and rain and the fine undercoat keeps the sheep warm. Kemp keeps the staple open and perpendicular to the body of the sheep. This protects the sheep even further from wind and rain and lets even more air in to the staple to keep the sheep warm. There is basically no crimp in the wool, and the color can vary over the body and over the staple.

Gute sheep still retain some of their primitive characteristics, one of which is *rooing*. This means that they naturally shed their wool once a year, usually in the spring or early summer. The fiber thins out and eventually breaks to pave the way for new growth. The different fiber types are rooed at different times. A shepherd who knows this can choose to shear the sheep at a specific time depending on which fiber type is being rooed.

⌐ Gute *wool from one individual, showing the long and strong overcoat, fine undercoat and kemp*

JW photo

⌐ *After flicking, a lot of kemp was stuck in the flick card*

JW photo

Josefin's Thoughts on Spinning

Because the kemp in the fleece keeps the staples open, *Gute* wool is light. I wanted to keep this lightness in the yarn that I spun. I could comb the fiber to make a strong yarn, but when I tried that I just enhanced the coarseness of the wool and it felt more like rope. That may have made a wonderfully strong and rustic rug yarn, but it was not what I was after. Since the three different fiber types are dependent on each other for their respective characteristics, I wanted to keep them together. Therefore I wanted to card them and spin a woolen yarn. For extra lightness I wanted to spin with low twist and 2-ply it. This resulted in a very pleasant sample with a rustic feeling. The felted swatch comes from a 10×10 cm woven sample. I love how the yarn felted—very evenly and with a nice touch to it.

To tease the wool before carding I flick carded the tip and cut ends. When I looked at the staples after flick carding I

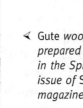

⌐ Gute *wool samples prepared for an article in the Spring 2019 issue of* Spin Off *magazine*

JW photo

saw something interesting. I found a lot less kemp in the flicked staples, especially at the cut end. This means that the kemp alone had been shed. If you look at the picture with all the staples in length order you can see the shedding point (the rise) at around 2 cm from the cut end.

What you see here is the cut end of the kemp is now in the flick card. Left in the staple was the rooed end and the tip end, both thinly tapered rather than straight angle cut. This means that the yarn would be less itchy than a *Gute* yarn with the cut ends in the yarn. Why? Well, a yarn is itchy if it makes the skin yield to the fiber. If instead the fiber yields to the surface of the skin, the yarn doesn't itch. Since the kemp ends are thinly tapered, the fibers will yield to the skin. By all means, this is still a rustic yarn that is itchier than, say, a *Merino* yarn, but the yarn I spun is surprisingly comfortable against my skin.

After having flicked the staples I carded rolags. *Gute* wool is wonderful to card. It feels light and airy, but still rustic. There is sort of a fudge-like feeling to carding this wool—slow but still smooth. There was a lot of kemp waste on the floor after I had carded the flicked staples. The kemp has quite a prominent medulla (the central core of the fiber, consisting of air-filled cells) and therefore breaks easily.

I wanted a yarn that had as much air as possible in it. I also wanted a yarn that would resemble the function of the

⌐ Gute *rolags*

JW photo

⋏ Gute *rolags (left) and Low-twist 2-ply woolen spun from hand-carded rolags*

JW photos

⋏ Gute *(left) and* Gotland *yarns compared. While* Gotland *sheep have been bred from* Gute, *the wool characteristics are quite different. The kemp of the* Gute *wool keeps the fiber lighter and more open, making the* Gotland *wool much more dense*

JW photo

⋏ *Elvis the* Gute *lamb with his mother and shepherdess Carina Josefsson*

Courtesy of Carina Josefsson

wool on the sheep as much as possible—strong and durable, yet still light and airy. Therefore I spun the carded rolags with longdraw at a low ratio for a low twist yarn. The longdraw captures a lot of air between the fibers and the low twist makes sure the air isn't squeezed out in a tight twist. The result was a remarkably light and airy yarn that is still strong and has a really rustic feeling.

Sara's Thoughts on Knitting

I was very excited to try out the *Gute* yarn, not only because Josefin's handspun was the only way for me to get my hands on prepared yarn, but because of the long history of this breed. Imagine a yarn that would have been used in the time of Vikings! Here in the Western Hemisphere, the only indigenous sheep are Bighorn

⋏ *Sara's knitted and felted swatches (left) and Josefin's woven and felted swatch*

SW/JW photos

sheep that crossed the Bering land bridge from Siberia as long as 750,000 years ago. These sheep were hunted for their horns and meat, but were never really used extensively for their skins, and not at all of their wool.

The *Gute* swatches were enjoyable to knit. The yarn is indeed light, and although rustic in its feel, quite compelling as a finished product for felting. I wasn't tempted to think of it as a yarn for jackets or hats, even though I'm sure it would be amazingly durable. It is, quite frankly, way too scratchy for my taste.

Finding *Gute* fleece is challenging, as you will discover if you do an online search. It can sometimes be found on Etsy. Your best luck in Sweden will be at wool festivals and craft fairs, and you may need to search for individual shepherds ahead of a trip. I was able to find a *Gute* lamb fleece from a fall sheering on the Ullförmedlingen site (*https://ullformedlingen.se/*), and the shepherdess was willing to ship it to the US (shipping was about 3 times the cost of the fleece) While raw, it is extremely clean with very little vegetable matter, and is full of curly locks.

Since I had to process this fleece myself to make knitting yarn, I can confirm Josefin's observations on kemp are important. I lost at least 60% of the weight of the fleece when the kemp was removed, so you need to take that into account when purchasing raw fleece to end up with enough yarn for your project. In addition, you might ask the shepherdess if the sheep were shorn specifically for hand spinning. Mine was not, so there were quite a number of second cuts, further reducing the final quantity of yarn. In my view, it was well worth the effort to have this rare breed to work with. Because of its truly rustic nature, my yarn will become part of an inkle-woven band rather than a knitted garment.

There really is no call for a commercial yarn from this sheep at this time, and because it remains reasonably rare, you are likely going to have to spin your own if you are interested in trying it out.

Härjedal

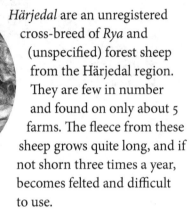

Härjedal are an unregistered cross-breed of *Rya* and (unspecified) forest sheep from the Härjedal region. They are few in number and found on only about 5 farms. The fleece from these sheep grows quite long, and if not shorn three times a year, becomes felted and difficult to use.

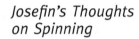

⅄ *Rya type locks from the 75% Härjedal/25% Åsen crossbred lamb Chanel*

JW photo

Josefin's Thoughts on Spinning

At the 2019 Swedish fleece championships I dug my hands into a fleece I felt an urgent need to spin. It was a 75% *Härjedal*/25% *Åsen* fleece from the lamb Chanel in a beautiful array of browns and light greys of rya type. I wanted to spin the fleece in a way where I could preserve as much of the color variation as possible. I divided the fleece into four piles of colors ranging from light rose grey to chocolate. I teased the locks with combs and removed most of the outercoat. I then hand-carded the undercoat and spun it into a light and airy yarn with English longdraw. My idea for the yarn is to use it in stranded colorwork knitting.

In this mainly undercoat yarn I was able to emphasize the main characteristics softness, color variation, and rusticity. I combed and saved the outercoat and

⅄ *Hand-carded rolags of mostly undercoat*

JW photo

⅄ *Spindle-spun* Harjedäl

JW photo

spun worsted into a strong warp yarn with a suspended spindle. In this yarn I was able to show the strength, shine and color variation of the outercoat.

Sara's Thoughts on Knitting

WOW! Can I get more of this? This may replace *Finull* as my favorite from Sweden. It makes me very sad to know that there are so few of this breed, and that they are so difficult to source. The fact that this particular combination of breeding has made an appearance at the Swedish fleece championships is a good sign, but crafters are a long way from being able to rely on its availability.

All of the credit here goes to Josefin's skills in separating the under- and outercoat fibers. I worked with the undercoat, not only soft and supple as a knitting yarn, but a gorgeous cocoa color with white highlights. I don't have enough to make anything with this yarn beyond a swatch, and will have to wait my turn to find more fleece, but this one is absolutely worth looking for.

⅄ *Swatch of Josefin's handspun* Harjedäl

SW photo

What impressed me in addition to the amazing softness was the very fine halo around the yarn. This persisted into the swatch, but the fibers are not so long that they obscure the stitches. It almost has the look of a fabric that was slightly brushed to raise the nap and slightly full the fibers. I'm guessing this would make amazing felt, but don't want to lose the character that was achieved by spinning to accentuate the white highlights. I realize I'm gushing, but the color mélange achieved in the knitted swatch is spectacular.

Helsingefår

Once a very common sheep in north-central Sweden, *Helsingefår* are now part of the group of breeds considered endangered. They are one of the so-called "forest" sheep, preferring pasturage with trees so that they can eat the bark. As good foragers,

Courtesy of Anna Lithner

they are popular for small farms where they help keep the landscape open while also providing meat and wool. From the *Swedish Fibre* site we get this information, "What's unique about the *Helsingefår* sheep is that it's quite common that the sheep have teat-like outgrowths on their throats. The Swedish word for these is 'skillingar.' Nobody really knows the function of these appendages but it's considered to be a sign of an "older sheep breed.'"

These sheep are double-coated, and like many others of the heritage sheep, have a variety of fiber types within a single fleece. The fleece also varies widely in color. Yarn spun from their fleece is often very glossy, and can be quite soft.

Josefin's Thoughts on Spinning

I didn't have any *Helsinge* wool, but after a quick search I found a fellow spinner and shepherdess of *Helsinge* sheep. She sent me some light brown quite fine locks of one of her ewes. The staples were of mainly finull and vadmal type. The main characteristics of the wool I worked with were the softness, the colors and the crimp.

I wanted to keep the softness and the loft in the staples. Therefore I teased and hand-carded the wool into rolags and made a 2-ply yarn with English longdraw. The rolags turned out very fuzzy and very clingy. Perhaps

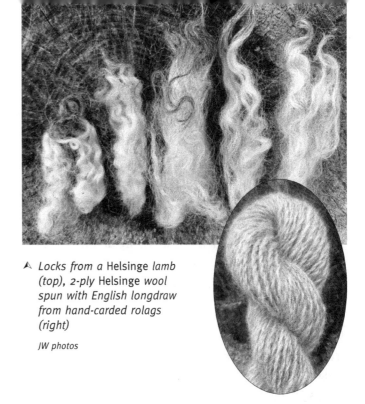

⋏ *Locks from a* Helsinge *lamb (top),* 2-ply Helsinge *wool spun with English longdraw from hand-carded rolags (right)*

JW photos

they would behave differently if the air was a bit less dry. Because of the fuzz I spun the yarn with more twist than I usually do to get a yarn with a decent stitch definition.

Sara's Thoughts on Knitting

I had three examples of *Helsinge* yarn to test knit and they were all very different from one another. This gave me an interesting opportunity to take a close look at how the breed performs depending on how it is handled in the spinning process. I've listened to Josefin talk about the "superpower of the fleece," and working with this yarn gave me a little more insight into what she means. While she has a much better understanding of the fleece characteristics from the way she works through all of the

⋏ *Handspun from batt (left), selected fiber handspun (center), mill spun (right)*

SW photo

processing and spinning, having three really different yarns made the light bulb come on.

The first yarn was handspun from a batt processed from the whole fleece. While it has a lovely silver-grey color, the fiber itself is very rough and dry. The other two are reasonably dry as well, so I'm assuming this is somewhat characteristic of the breed. Given that they are forest sheep prone to subsisting on a diet that includes tree bark, I can imagine that they don't produce a huge amount of lanolin. From this discussion I'm sure you won't be surprised that I didn't enjoy knitting with this particular yarn. It was exceptionally rough—beyond rustic.

Josefin's handspun was carefully selected from the finull and vadmal-type parts of the fleece from a ewe. While she thought they were soft, the yarn itself feels reasonably rustic to me. In this case, her processing did make a very lofty yarn that knits well and gives good stitch definition. It also is a lovely color (because *Helsinge* are multi-colored, it is possible to get quite a variety in yarns).

The third sample is a mill-spun *Helsinge* from Winterliagården. It is very different than either of the handspun examples first and foremost because it has a much tighter twist giving the yarn itself a much more compact shape. That also means it a little more dense than the other two and so I felt like I needed to try something a little different. For this swatch I threw in a couple of cables.

Like all of these rustic yarns, however, the halo of fibers does diminish the impact of the cable somewhat. Compared to a cable on *Finull*, for example, the *Helsinge* cable is subtle. That could be used to advantage in some designs.

Even though the mill-spun *Helsinge* is a bit softer than even Josefin's handspun, it still is in the "rustic" category. The dryness also is a disadvantage, so I'm not certain how I'd use this fiber. Maybe a blend with *Finull*?

Jämtlandsfår

Jämtland sheep produce good wool and meat. Unlike most of the heritage breeds that are generally composed of a single breed type, these sheep are a purposeful cross-breed

‹ Jämtlandsfår *sheep*

Courtesy of Yarns & Barns, UllForum Spinneri

⌃ Jämtlandsfår *fleece*

SW photo (bottom)

⌃ *Whole-year staples of unwashed long* Jämtland *wool*

Dan Waltin, photographer

of *Merino*, introduced in 2004, and *Svea*. *Svea* also are cross-bred; a mix of *Finull* and *Texel*. *Jämtlandsfår* were presented at the World Merino Conference in 2010 as a new breed, found primarily in Jämtland province and further north.

Josefin's Thoughts on Spinning

Jämtland sheep are bred mainly for meat and wool, with emphasis on wool for industrial spinning. The wool is beautifully fine and consistent over the body of the sheep and over the staple. The shepherdess I buy my fleece from covers her sheep and shears once a year, resulting in around 6 inch long, clean and uniform staples. These are a dream to prepare and spin.

For me, *Jämtland* wool is crimpy, shiny and extremely soft. I spun my first few *Jämtland* fleeces worsted from hand-combed tops. These were very bouncy and uniform and a joy to spin. One day, though, I decided to try to spin flicked staples from the fold. At that moment an epiphany came to me— this is how these locks want to be spun. Spinning from the fold gave the yarn that extra bounce

⌃ Jämtland *yarn from flick carded staples spun from the fold on a supported spindle*

JW photo

and aura that it had always longed for. The folded fibers came into the drafting triangle from a wider angle, creating a more airy yarn. Furthermore, the fibers desperately wanted to unfold, keeping them striving outwards and adding to that airiness. Spinning from the fold is now my go-to method for long *Jämtland* staples. Shorter staples I would card and spin woolen.

There is no wonder that *Jämtland* wool is so popular among knitters, hand spinners, spinning mills and manufacturers. The softness, fineness and uniformity together with the lovely shine make *Jämtland* fleece very attractive. Despite the softness and the initial satisfaction this wool is not on the top of my personal list—it is too perfect and I am more attracted to wool with more variation.

Sara's Thoughts on Knitting

Jämtlandsfår yarn is turning up in commercial yarns across Sweden, the most widely distributed currently being *Yarns & Barns* from UllForum Spinnery. Most of this yarn is in the natural colors of the sheep, but dyed yarns are becoming more available.

I swatched first with the *Yarns & Barns* dark brown 2-ply on US size 4 (3.5mm) needles. The swatch was beautifully soft, and has a nice drape. Based on the swatch measurements I cast on for a winter headband with the remainder of the dark skein and a pale grey (almost white) skein of the same (undyed) yarn.

These yarns work well for stranding. I would describe them as almost "sticky" as there is never a problem of splitting the ply, even working with very sharply pointed needles (my own preference). What I did notice, however, are quite a number of very minor imperfections in the yarn in the form of breaks or blooms in the singles of the dark brown. Even though the plies do not separate, at the point of the breaks the yarn tends to fluff out a little, giving the knitting a bit of a rustic look. I like the fact that these little imperfections give the yarn almost a handspun look, but am concerned that in a garment like a sweater, those breaks could cause the garment not to wear well.

I talked to the mill spinners about this, and they are aware of the issue and plan to address it in improving their production. As part of that discussion, I told them

⋀ *Josefin's knitting project—a shawl from her hand-combed and worsted spun lace yarn of* Jämtland *wool*

Dan Waltin, photographer

⋀ *Headband knitted from two natural colors of* Jämtland *from Yarns & Barns*

Modeled by Leah Nappi, Lauren Nappi, photographer

that in some respects I find this a feature that might even be brought to the attention of knitters as a potential positive. The slight irregularity is not offensive, and with a little testing to see if it will stand up to regular wear, it could give garments a unique character that you won't find with yarn from a different mill. In fact, irregularity is a feature I find rather common with yarn from Swedish mini-mills, either from variations in thickness within a skein, or slubs and breaks in others. My opinion is that these yarns are unique and special, and while I could find one that will give me identical stitches throughout a garment, my preference is for the character I find prevalent in Swedish yarns.

Klövsjöfår

Klövsjö sheep originate from a small village in Jämtland County. According to the Swedish breed association (Föreningen Svenska Allmogefår) in the 1990s, there were only two flocks in the area surrounding Klövsjö village, kept by an elderly lady who had inherited them from her father. Her father reportedly was given the sheep as a wedding present from his mother.

⋏ Klövsjö*får sheep (left) and lambs (right)*

©*Vuokko Hogland, photographer*

⋏ Klövsjö *staples*

JW photo

These are double-coated sheep, with long, lustrous wool, generally in black, white, and grey, although some brown fleece can be found.

Josefin's Thoughts on Spinning

The *Klövsjö* wool I have handled has been of mostly rya type—long and shiny fibers with lots of outercoat. The fibers

⋏ *Two-ply yarn from one black and one silver single*

JW photo

themselves are almost straight. To me it is the perfect candidate for warp, rya knots, or embroidery yarn. It is also a good wool type to separate into undercoat and outercoat to spin separately—a softer yarn for knitting from the undercoat and a strong and shiny weaving yarn from the outercoat. In the yarn I spun for Sara I wanted to emphasize the shine, the color variations and the strength.

First I separated the black and silver locks to prepare and spin them separately. I chose to use the fiber types together in a strong and shiny yarn. I combed the locks and spun them worsted. I then made a 2-ply using, one black single and one silver single together.

Sara's Thoughts on Knitting

I located a small farm in the southeast of Sweden where Vuokko and her husband are raising *Klövsjö* and running a lovely B&B (she will even teach you to spin if you stay there for a visit). She knitted a couple of swatches of her yarn to show me what it looks like, and I went head over heals for a batch she had carded with random swaths of silvery-white in the black. Knitted, the fabric resembles an ikat weaving with the white edging into the black in small patterns that almost look as though they were space-dyed. If you are a hand-spinner, you can get pretty exotic looking yarn by treating the fleece like a multi-colored "braid," and controlling the location of the various colors of fleece. The alternative Josefin chose was to make tweed by plying two colors together in equal amounts. Either way, this fleece is another one with multiple possibilities.

The results from both Josefin's and Vuokko's hand-spun were pretty similar. At 16wpi, Josefin's yarn made a fine, dense fabric with alternating bands of dark and variegated patterns. The yarn has a nice hand and a somewhat rustic feel. It is strong, and robust, and would

⋏ Josefin's handspun (top), handspun from
Vuokko Hogland (SheepShopen) (bottom)

SW photos

⋏ Two-ply weaving yarn of hand-combed
and worsted spun Leicester wool (right).

JW photo

work well for a sweater or heavier outerwear. Worked in stockinette, the right side has a very smooth feel, with the silvery fibers giving the fabric an almost slippery feel. The bloom of fiber ends on the purl side might be considered scratchy. Working with Vuokko's handspun was really fun. She purposely took the various colors of the fleece and spaced them so that an apparently random series of stripes or pools of black and white occurred. I wanted to keep knitting just to see what would happen next. Vuokko's yarn was also spun to take advantage of the rustic nature of *Klövsjö* with bits of thick and thin to add to the texture. I love the versatility of this breed, and although not perfectly soft, it is very appealing.

Leicester (Swedish Leicester)

⋏ Leicester *ewe*

SW photo

Leicester sheep, originally bred in England, were brought to Sweden in the mid-1700s by agricultural pioneer Jonas Alströmer. Some were interbred with *Gutefår* on Gotland Island resulting in offspring with white wool. After nearly 300 years, these sheep have been bred and acclimatized to Sweden to the point where it can be considered a Swedish breed on its own.

Josefin's Thoughts on Spinning

Leicester locks are quite compact with nearly all outercoat; very shiny and very strong. There is a lot of resemblance between Swedish *Gotland* wool and *Swedish Leicester* wool in this respect. My experience is that *Leicester* wool is a little less fussy and easier to process and spin than *Gotland* wool.

To capture the essence of the shine, the strength and the silkiness I chose to comb my *Leicester* locks and spin worsted. It resulted in a freakishly strong and shiny yarn that I used as a warp yarn and later for rya knots.

Sara's thoughts on Knitting

I knit a swatch of Josefin's 2-ply that she used for the knots on her chair cushions, and I agree that in the hand it does resemble *Gotland* quite a bit. It has great shine and quite a bit of excess of the fuzzy halo that tends toward the rustic side. I'm not sure that this is true, but it also seems to have a bit more lanolin in the fibers than some of the other breeds (Swedish sheep are a bit on the "dry" side with less lanolin than I'm used to—in washing fleece it's important to keep that in mind to prevent stripping it all out). This is another one of the breeds that I think needs more mixing of its fleece with other types to come up with the perfect knitting yarn.

⋏ Swatch knitted from Josefin's 2-ply handspun yarn

SW photo

▲ Roslags sheep
Courtesy of Anna Lisa Osberg

➢ Roslags lambs
Courtesy of Petra Aschberg

▲ Staples of Roslag wool

➢ Two-ply woolen spun yarn from hand-carded Roslag locks
JW photos

Roslagsfår

Once the most common sheep in the Roslagen area north of Stockholm in Upplands Province, these sheep were reduced to only a single flock by the early 1900s. Nils Dahlbeck and Lars Englund identified *Roslags* sheep in the early 1990s in northern Roslagen. They remain one of the most endangered domesticated sheep in Sweden.

Mostly white, black with white spots, or speckled black and white, these small sheep are double-coated with curly or wavy wool. The wool is a rya type. *Roslags* are mostly white, black with white spots, or speckled black and white. These sheep are sometimes called carpet sheep because of their long, straight guard hair and a thick undercoat. This type of wool can be spun, but does not felt well.

Historically the wool was spun, woven, knitted and nålbound for household textiles and clothing. Textiles in the collections of the Upplands Museum (Upplands-museet) in Uppsala contain wool that is identical to that found on current *Roslagsfår*.

Josefin's thoughts on Spinning

I was able to get *Roslag* staples at a wool festival. Most of them had quite soft and airy undercoat and strong and shiny outercoat. The staples were almost straight. The shine, airiness and versatility were the characteristics I wanted to emphasize. The staples put me in the same spinning mode as the *Åsen* wool I had and I decided to prepare and spin these in a similar fashion. I teased and hand-carded them into rolags and spun woolen with

English longdraw into a 2-ply yarn with low twist. It resulted in a light and airy yarn with a soft but somewhat rustic touch.

Sara's Thoughts on Knitting

I have to agree with Josefin's assessment that the *Roslag* fiber produces a rustic yarn, but I didn't find it very soft. It is, however, very strong, and for that reason I can understand why it's a good choice for nålbinding. Not only does it hold up well when pulled repeatedly through the nålbound stitches, it doesn't break as easily as some other yarns. The ability to resist breaking and to hold up to abrasion are very good characteristics for this use. Also, the fact that it doesn't felt easily would be an advantage.

▲ Swatch from Josefin's handspun Roslagsfår
SW photo

My skills at nålbinding aren't good enough to show, so I did knit a swatch. On its own, I don't think it would work at all for garments worn next to the skin. Its resistance to felting might make it a candidate for outerwear. I do think it might make a great addition to a yarn with fragile, soft or stretchy characteristics (such as alpaca or angora) to make something like a sock yarn you could want to resist abrasion.

▲ Rya rug circa 1930, possibly from the Upplands region (east coast of Sweden)

Courtesy of the Nordiska museet (NM.0187701), Elisabeth Eriksson, photographer

Ryafår

Rya is both the name of a sheep breed and a descriptor for a very robust and shiny yarn composed of both under- and outercoat. The breed originated from a combination of Swedish and Norwegian landrace breeds such as Norwegian *Spæsau*, and can be found in northern and central Sweden, mainly in Dalarna Province. Like others of the conservation breeds, this type was nearly extinct by the early 1900s in spite of its popularity for use in the so-called Rya Rugs (a wooly, shaggy rug). Because of this use, the sheep are often called "Swedish Carpet Wool" Sheep.

▲ Rya *sheep (left), gold medalist* Rya *fleece in the 2019 Swedish fleece championships (unwashed) (right)*

Courtesy of Sven Sillé, Ekenäs hantverk (left), JW photo (right)

Most *Rya* are white, but brown, grey and black individuals are not uncommon. The wool fibers are about 6" in length on a lamb, growing to 12" or longer on an adult. About half of the fleece is the hair, or outer coat, which is lustrous and has a well-defined crimp.

Josefin's Thoughts on Spinning

Like *Jämtland* and *Finull* sheep, *Rya* sheep are bred mainly for their wool as first and foremost a weaving yarn. *Rya* yarn is also an excellent fiber to add to sock yarn for strength.

Handling *Rya* fleece is a joy as well as a challenge. The staples are fascinating to work with and at the same time a bit cumbersome when it comes to the length. For

▲ *3-ply sock yarn from Rya/ mohair blend (60/40). Worsted spun on a supported spindle from hand-combed top*

JW photo

▲ *Two-ply worsted spun yarn from hand-combed top, intended as an embroidery yarn*

JW photo

both carding and combing you need to pull your tools far enough apart to separate the fibers between them, otherwise you will end up with loops and a tangled mess.

An obvious choice would be to comb the long locks, either as they are or the outercoat only, and spin them into a worsted yarn. Weaving is the technique that comes to mind, either for warp or for strong and shiny rya knots. Since the undercoat is also quite long, it is fully possible to card the staples as well. The different lengths help keeping the fibers together, resulting in lovely rolags where the outercoat binds them together with its shiny fibers. With this preparation woolen spinning is definitely an option. Of course you can also separate the fiber types and prepare and spin them in different manners.

I am experimenting with a sock yarn of adult mohair. I added the *Rya* rolags (carded into the mohair) for extra strength.

Sara's Thoughts on Knitting

As drawn as I was to the creamy vanilla-white hand-spun yarn sample I was given, *Rya* is not a knitting yarn—at least not on its own. After casting onto my needles and knitting a row, its slippery surface and springy nature immediately made me think of a warp yarn for weaving.

I was working with a 2-ply, which didn't want to stay together on the needles. Because the *Rya* locks are long and very much like hair, they don't have the fuzzy/sticky character of a fleece like *Gotland*, so the plies don't remain attached to one another. I did a very small swatch just to have the example, and was somewhat frustrated by the fact that the yarn itself is absolutely gorgeous, with a beautiful surface sheen. Clearly it needs to be mixed with something else to be useful for knitting, and while its robust character could certainly benefit a more fragile wool, I am hopeful that not all of the shine will get lost in mixing.

In fact, *Rya* is often mixed with other fibers to add strength and resiliency. Because those locks are so long

▲ *Examples of z-spun and swatch from Wålstedts yarns*

SW photos

and slippery, however, it's not easy to control, and it has a habit of clogging up spinning machinery. My introduction to this at one of the mini-mills came from one of the master spinners working atop one of the spinning machines, pulling fiber out from one such clog and muttering under her breath, "I hate *Rya!*"

Another of the mills that has managed to make *Rya* the centerpiece of some of their yarns is Wålstedts Ullspinneri. *Rya* is an important component of their z-ply yarn for two-end knitting, and their machinery has been developed specifically to handle locks up to 30 cm in length (nearly one foot). This makes a difference in that they are able to make a yarn that has an amazingly hard twist that not only holds up to the manipulation required to work the stitches, but retains that gorgeous shine imparted by the *Rya* locks.

Svärdsjöfår

Svärdsjö is another of the landrace forest sheep from Dalarna province bred to subsist on limited pasturage in the summer and to survive in the forests in winter. While it is a distinct breed, *Svärdsjö* is also the name given to the common sheep of the Province, found primarily in white, although some are black with white markings.

Anna-Britta and Erland Johansson have a farm in Hillerboda Svärdsjö that has been in the family from

▲ *Swatch knit from hand-spun* Rya

SW photo

Courtesy of Nancy Wiklund

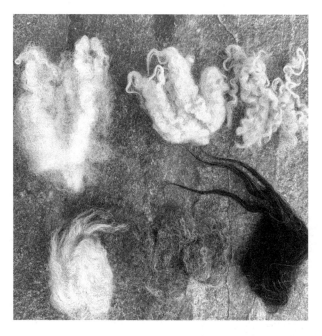

⅄ Locks from six different individuals of Svärdsjö *sheep. The lace yarn I sent to Sara came from the top middle sample*

JW photo

the 17th century, where these small sheep have 'always been around'. Anna-Britta remembers her grandmother preparing the skins and sewing leather sweaters as well as spinning knitting yarns.[2]

The softest parts of the fleece are often used for embroidery yarn as well as knitting, and may be called "German Shawl Yarn."

Josefin's Thoughts on Spinning

Having a tuft of *Svärdsjö* wool in your hands is a joy. The staples are curly-crispy with lots of elasticity and a very special shine. No, I would say that *Svärdsjö* more glistens than shines. Another characteristic of *Svärdsjö* wool is that it tends to have a special smell to it apart from the regular sheep smell. Somewhat… cheesy. Not offensive, but different.

Just like wool from the other heritage breeds *Svärdsjö* wool is versatile and can range between rya and finull staple types. It has mainly fine fibers close to the finull range. Combing, carding, woolen or worsted spinning are all possible and give lovely results. The characteristics I wanted to emphasize in the wool I got was the shine, softness and crimp. I chose to spin a laceweight yarn from hand-carded rolags in a semi-worsted manner on a supported spindle. The fibers draft smoothly and are a joy to spin. I imagine an open lacework that shows the shine in the yarn while still being next-to-skin soft.

Sara's Thoughts on Knitting

I didn't actually reread Josefin's evaluation of *Svärdsjö* before picking it up to begin the test knit, but with it in hand, my first thought was…..lace! What she had sent me was very soft, but with a sufficiently robust feel that I thought a lacy springtime cardigan might emerge from this yarn. I did a small swatch with a simple two-row lace pattern, and I really love how it turned out.

This fiber slips between your fingers, and I understood right away what Josefin meant about it drafting easily. It has a wonderful texture, and is hearty without being the least bit scratchy. If fleece could play music, *Svärdsjö* would be spirited jazz.

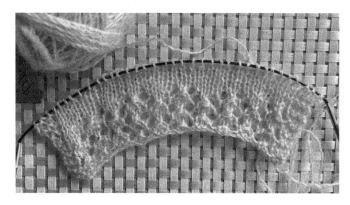

⅄ Lace swatch knit from Josefin's handspun Svärdsjo *yarn*

SW photo

△ Svea *lamb*

SW *photo*

△ Swatch from Texel

SW *photo*

Sveafår

Other than *Svea* being a component of *Jaämtlandsfår* you find few references to this breed in general information about Swedish sheep breeds. Even a search through the Ullförmedlingen site failed to turn up any available fleece. While this is not a rare or endangered breed, it does not seem to have a ready market at this time. I have only seen it listed as a breed yarn once, and not available outside of Sweden.

Tabacktorpsfår

The *Tabacktorps* sheep are named for the Tabacktorp farm in Värmland. There are few of these sheep remaining, and it isn't known if the fleece used to be more colored (they are mostly white now). These are very small forest sheep (40–60 pounds) and their fleece, while variable, is often soft and curly. *Tabacktorpsfår* have only been in the Gene Bank since 2014, and are not really a commercially viable breed at this time.

△ Tabacktorps sheep

Courtesy of Louise Westerberg (top) and Eva Sköld (bottom)

Texel

Originally from the Netherlands, *Texel* sheep were imported to Sweden via Denmark and crossbred with *Finull* sheep to produce the *Svea* breed.

Texel produce a fine, dense fleece with moderately soft wool said to be good for knitwear and stockings.

Like many of the breeds found in Sweden, *Texel* fleece is often mixed with other breed fleece to create yarn with specific properties. The breed also has been crossed with *finull* to create the *Svea* breed. *Svea* and *Merino* were then crossed to develop the *Jämtlandfår*.

Sara's Thoughts on Knitting

Texel yarn is something I didn't expect to come across. I had never seen it referenced for anything other than being a component of the *Jämtland* breed via *Svea*. On its own, it's not considered a heritage breed, and isn't endangered. It was a surprise to find it at the Stenkyrka mini-mill on Gotland Island, and even though it's not a yarn they would regularly make, I thought it was worth giving it a try to see just what characteristics it might be contributing to these other breeds.

It's quite soft and its texture reminds me of unmercerized cotton—almost a spongy feel. Like so many of these yarns and breeds, this needs more exploration.

Värmlandsfår

Värmland sheep nearly disappeared from Sweden when more meaty breeds were introduced in the 18th and 19th centuries. The last flock of about 100 animals was located near the Norwegian border about 30 years ago and became part of the effort to preserve traditional breeds. As a conservation breed, these sheep have been carefully bred and now number around 4,000 in 170 flocks. This makes them the largest of the conservation breeds and a wonderful example of thoughtful animal husbandry.

△ Värmland sheep

Courtesy of Gammeldags and Hyltorna Farm

These sheep are quite small, have a double coat and the wool is considered to be medium-to-coarse in texture. As can be seen from the staples, there are quite a variety of wool types, from long dual coated staples, to both fleece with predominantly outercoat, or predominantly undercoat. There are a variety of natural colors including white, brown, grey, beige and black, and some of the sheep are spotted.

Josefin's Thoughts on Spinning

There are two different lines of *Värmland* sheep. The traditional has a lot of undercoat with a few strands of outercoat. The staples are triangular in shape, and are open and airy and they produce a soft, silky and strong yarn.

Modern *Värmland* sheep include some that were crossed with Old Norwegian *Spæl* rams and perhaps also Swedish *Rya* when they were rediscovered 30 years ago. This produced wool with long outercoat and some kemp.

Since the staples have a variety of characteristics, the *Värmland* wool is very versatile. I can use different preparation methods and spin a wide variety of yarns from silky soft lace yarn to robust sock yarn and even rug yarn.

In my experience this wool is very lightweight. When you look at the staples you see a broad base with lots of air. This also makes the wool very easy to spin.

Finally, the array of colors provides infinite possibilities.

With this variety of staple and fiber types, you can process and spin *Värmland* in many different ways—fiber types separated, together, and with different tools and spinning techniques.

Longer staples of *Värmland* wool can be combed either with both fiber types together or by separating undercoat from outercoat. I spun a combed top with short draw into a strong and shiny yarn.

In another fleece with different staple types the fleece was separated into two piles—one for long and wavy

staples and another for the shorter and crimpier staples. The latter were carded—outercoat and undercoat together—and spun with a medieval spindle and distaff into a very airy and light yarn.

In order to preserve as much of the color variation from a fleece with light silvery-grey in the cut end and honey-dipped tips, I flick carded the staples and spun them individually from the cut end.

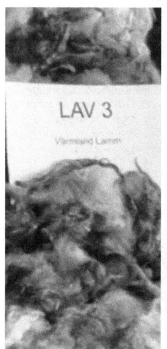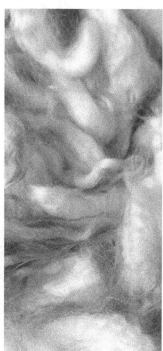

⋏ *Raw fleece (left); traditional (right)*
JW photo

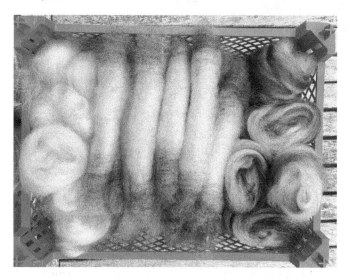

⋏ *Outercoat hand-combed bird's nests (left and right). Undercoat hand-carded rolags (middle).*
JW photo

⋖ *Värmland Staples*
JW photo

⋏ Yarn spun with short draw from hand-combed top using outercoat only (left); Värmland wool with lots of undercoat is lovely to card and spin with long draw. The skein here is undercoat, carded, and spun with a long draw on a Navajo spindle into a lightweight and airy singles yarn (right)

JW photos

⋏ Commercially spun Värmlands yarn (bottom) and knitted swatch (top)

SW photos

⋏ Outercoat and undercoat carded together (left); flick carded staples spun individually from the cut end (right)

JW photos

Sara's Thoughts on Knitting

Both Josefin and I have done a bit of knitting with *Värmland* wool and have found it useful for different types of projects. The only commercially produced yarn I found was from *Framgården* at a wool festival. This small producer sells only onsite at the mill or at wool festivals at present.

I split a skein of 2-ply in half and dyed one-half dark red. It turned out to be a lovely shade, but the depth of shade was a little too similar to the brown, so it didn't stand out very well for stranded knitting. That being said, it was very nice to work with—a very sturdy yarn with quite a bit of halo (you can see the fuzzy bits sticking up even after wet blocking). Because of the reasonably tight twist of this yarn, the stitches are distinct, and have nice definition. Unfortunately, my dye choice was too close in tone to the natural color, making pattern differentiation poor. This is definitely a yarn I'd like to return to if and when I can find more, particularly given the multiple possibilities of natural shades.

Josefin was able to control the outcome of her yarn by carefully choosing and separating the various fibers from her fleece. In consequence, some of her yarns are softer than the commercial version. Others turned out to be more rugged, and the obvious value of this particular sheep breed is the ability to produce a large variety of yarns without blending with different wools.

This weaving sample for a pillow top (next page) is a very good example of using the properties of different wools to create yarn with a specific purpose:

- The warp is *Shetland*—strong and durable.
- The knots are *Swedish Leicester*—soft to the touch
- The wefts (dark brown) are *Värmland* wool—robust to withstand beating in.

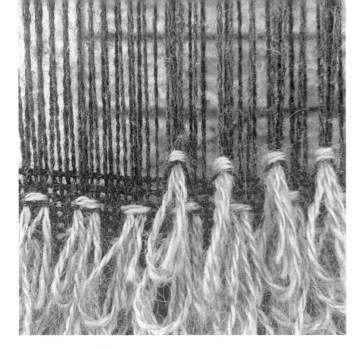

⋏ *Weaving sample for a pillow top with dark brown wefts*
JW photo

Josefin also created two different yarns for mitts and mittens. The mitts (below) were wheel-spun yarn from flick-carded staples.[3] The mittens were made with z-plied *Värmland* wool and worked in the two-end (Tvåändsstickning) technique. The close-up image of the mitten provides a good illustration of the yarn character.

FLAX TO LINEN

⋏ *Flax flowers*
D. Gordon E. Robertson, photographer

There is significant evidence that flax was grown in Sweden from prehistoric times, and at least initially was probably used primarily for oil (linseed oil) and for its medicinal properties. From the Viking era into the Middle Ages and up until the beginning of the 19th century, flax was processed for thread that was used in making linen fabrics. An interesting fact about flax is that the lovely blue flower blooms only for one day.

The primary flax-growing area was in Hälsingland. A flax mill dating from the early 19th century has been relocated from Hälsingland to the outdoor museum Skansen in Stockholm, where it is powered by a water wheel. Museum staff process flax in late summer to give visitors an idea of the work involved in taking flax from the plant to weaving thread.

⋏ *Mitts from wheel spun Väemlands yarn (upper left), mittens of z-ply Värmlands wool (upper right), close-up of mitten (lower)*

Dan Waltin and Josefin Waltin, photographers

⋏ *Processing flax circa 1900-1920*
Courtesy of the Nordiska museet (NM.0034109), Okänd Fotograf

In order to understand just how labor-intensive it would have been to grow and process flax and to spin it, weave it, and make something like a shirt from that fabric, a group of archeologists from the University of Southern Denmark and the staff of the Ribe Viking Centre undertook a project to reproduce a shirt found in the 11th century settlement at Viborg Søndersø. Flax was planted in 2010 and harvested in 2011. After rippling, retting, breaking, scutching and heckling, the most intensive part of the work began with 3 spinners working independently to give the researchers an idea of the range of time needed to spin the needed 753 grams of thread. Very skilled hand spinners produced the fine thread using a suspended spindle and portable distaff, and the fabric was woven on a warp weighted loom. The spinning and weaving took 85% of the total time for the project, and altogether, depending on the skill of the spinner in particular, the total time ranged from 354 to 598 hours to spin the thread.

The other part of the experiment that was illuminating was the amount of plant material required to produce the linen thread from the flax plant. In the breaking process alone, between 70 and 82% of the material is lost. This part of flax processing separates the fibers from the straw. In the scutching and heckling, more short and broken fibers are removed. On average, by weight, 50% of the material again is lost to the process. The final calculation was that 21kg (just over 46 pounds) of fresh plants need to be harvested to create 753 g (1.66 pounds)

of thread for a piece of fabric just under 2.5m in length and 60cm in width (2.7 yds/24").[4] When you consider the amount of effort needed to produce linen for a family, or the extensive amount of materials and time to weave the sails for a Viking sailing ship, it becomes quickly clear how important textile production was in our early history.

There is little written about knitting with linen, although you can find examples of stockings and gloves knitted in linen in museum collections. There is a skill involved in knitting with linen because it is slippery, making it that much more impressive to find these items worked at an extremely fine gauge. Another place it occurs in Swedish knitting is in the cuffs of mittens from Dalarna province. It is used sparingly for fine decorative details.

In the 19th century with the introduction of cotton (both cheaper to acquire and faster to get from plant to thread), flax production virtually came to a halt. Still, in the relatively short duration of its popularity, Sweden developed a reputation for the production of high quality linens. Although flax is no longer cultivated widely in Sweden, there are still factories producing linen fabric, and at least three mills still producing linen yarn: Växbo, Holma-Helsinglands, and Borgs.

Weavers likely are familiar with all 3 of these companies as they ship internationally. Knitters also will have a reasonably easy time finding smaller amounts (skeins) of linen yarn for projects both within and outside of Sweden.

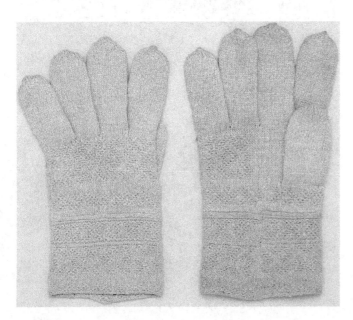

Lace gloves, late 19th century

Courtesy of Nordiska museet (NM.0073933), Mona-Lisa Djerf, photographer

Linen knit into a two-end knitting mitten cuff in the style of Dalarna province

SW photo

FOOTNOTES

1. I have heard from some US shepherds that bringing *Gotland* sheep to a new country has challenges. The traditional diet for these sheep is high in chromium from seaweed, and newly introduced sheep need mineral supplements added to their feed. It would be interesting to learn if through years of adaptation in other climates whether or not the wool itself changes in character

2. From the Föreningen Svenska Allmogefår website listing for *Svärdsjö* (https://allmogefar.se/svaerdsjoefar).

3. The pattern for these mitts can be found in the Fall 2019 issue of *Spin Off* magazine

4. Ejstrud, Bo (ed.), From Flax to Linen: Experiments with flax at Ribe Viking Centre. 2011, Esbjerg, Denmark, University of Southern Denmark

4 Visiting Sweden

While not a comprehensive overview of everything fiber in Sweden, here are some highlights of the larger cities/areas you may be lucky enough to visit. This is an always changing landscape of businesses, and we hope to be as up-to-date as possible on the website, *aknitwizard.com*. There we will endeavor to add and delete shop information as we learn of changes. Think of this guide for crafters as the "one potato chip" travel guide—you can't have just one. There is so much to see and do in Sweden that you'll want to consult other resources for hotels and restaurants, hiking and camping, and the many other museums that weren't included here. We didn't even try to cope with things like Midsummer festivals and Christmas markets, or the many local and regional crafts shops. Sweden is an adventure waiting to happen.

⋀ *Street in Gamla Stan, Stockholm*

Photo by Linus Mimietz on Unsplash

FINDING YARN IN STOCKHOLM

There are plenty of opportunities to increase your stash in Stockholm including craft shops as well as yarn stores. I've even found yarn in a couple of bookstores! Just like everywhere else, this is an ever-changing landscape, where new shops open, others change hands, and some close. The same can be said for the varieties of yarn that shops handle. Check shop websites as well as those for the local museums. You might find a knitting café, some classes or workshops, or maybe a festival that includes interesting textile activities. Also take a look at the *Sticka!* website for possible activities in and around the city that coincide with your trip dates (see Other Resources, Chapter 9).

The following listings are organized by neighborhood to make it easier to visit more locations efficiently, starting from the heart of the old town and expanding out from there. Stockholm is an easy city to negotiate by tram and bus, so make your visit there an adventure. With a multi-day pass (purchased at any of the stations), you can use all forms of transport for unlimited trips, and there will be no shortage of helpful assistance to get you on the right track.

Gamla Stan

Gamla Stan—the old city, dates back to the 13th century and is filled with cobbled walking streets and medieval alleyways, restaurants, tourist shops and charming architecture. It is a photographer's delight. It also is the location of the Nobel Museum, the Stockholm Cathedral and the 18th century Royal Palace.

If you are looking for souvenirs of traditional-style Swedish mittens, sweaters or socks, you will find them in some of the shops here. One style of mitten to look for is the Lovikka mitten, a type from northern Sweden where the makers actually hold a patent on that style. An authentic Lovikka mitten will be tagged with the patent seal (see pg. 20)

Orient yourself to locate the yarn shops here from the Nobel Museum at the top of the hill on the main square. From there, you are only a 2–3 minute walk from yarny goodness.

MAKERI 14

Köpmangatan 14

Makeri 14 is a small, cozy shop in the heart of the old town that has a singular focus—wool. The owner, Stephanie, is very particular in what she stocks because the space is limited, and she doesn't want to waste her time with products she doesn't feel are enjoyable to work with. She loves to work with wool, and so that is the focus of her carefully curated selection. The selection is international, changing, and does include one Swedish yarn—*UllRika* from Yarns & Barns (100% *Jämtland* wool). Be sure to buy enough for your project as shipping has become prohibitively expensive and small shops like this frequently do not operate web shops.

During your visit, be sure to ask about the next Stick Kafé (knitting get-together). Stephanie often supports regular meet-ups at a nearby pub where you will be welcomed to join other knitters and share your current projects.

STICKA BY MARIE VICTORIA

Österlånggatan 37

https://knitting.se

SW photos

This shop is sometimes confused with the *Sticka!* organization (the Swedish knitters' guild that has the purpose of connecting knitters together). Make no mistake; Marie Victoria's boutique is quite different from that, being a location to purchase her lovely hand-made knitwear, patterns, and a few exceptional skeins of yarn. She carries a limited selection based on what she is showing in her shop. This may include yarns by Yllet or Yarbo wool.

Marie Victoria is a delightful, enthusiastic ambassador for knitting, and it is unlikely that you will leave her shop empty-handed. If it isn't too busy, try to convince her to show you her first knitting project (she keeps in under the counter).

⌄ Inside of MAKERI 14

SW photos

⌄ Two of Marie Victoria's designs. The airy lightweight vest on the left pays homage to the traditional Kasung jacket with curly fleece locks for trim. She has used Gotland fleece hand-spun into an art yarn to decorate the neck edge.

SW photos

73

GALLERI YAMANASHI
Köpmantorget 1
http://galleri-yamanashi.com/

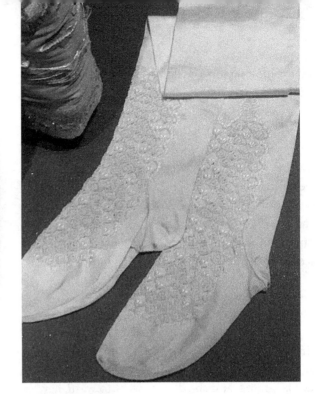

The art gallery
Yamanashi is definitely
worth checking out.
With a varied, chang-
ing program, there is
no guarantee that you
will find the focus on
knitting or yarn, but you

Courtesy of Galleri Yamanashi

undoubtedly will find something of interest. You are just
as likely to find embroidery from Denmark as Swedish
birch bark baskets or an exhibition of yarn from one of
the Swedish textile mills along with examples of traditional weaving, knitting and embroidery. In 2018
the Gallery had an exhibition featuring the wool of
Wålstedts Textilverkstad. Workshops often accompany
their exhibitions, and their website lists both past and
upcoming offerings.

Note: The Gallery is only open when exhibitions are installed there—
check their website for times.

Other things in Gamla Stan

The Royal Armory or *Livrustkammaren* (Slottsbacken 3)
is located on the back side of the Royal Palace at the foot
of Gamla Stan hill. Tucked away with its entry off of a car
park, it is easy to miss, but well worth the effort if you
have an interest in textiles and clothing. My favorite arti-
fact in the exhibition is a fashion doll or Pandora (page
14). This miniature early 17th century doll features perfect
replicas of Spanish fashion, including an appropriate
hairstyle. Pandora dolls were used as a method of sharing
fashion from one royal court to another, and were found
all over Europe and Scandinavia into the 19th century
when they began to be replaced by fashion magazines.

The exhibits show an interesting timeline of dress and
changing styles reflective of court fashion. While these
garments were not attainable by ordinary people, they

▲ *Fine hand-knit silk stockings at the*
Royal Armory Museum in Gamla Stan

SW photos

certainly were imitated and relied upon for changing
styles among all classes of society. There are several
examples of knitted stockings that may have been produced in distant workshops and imported to Sweden.

You will have no problem finding shops with interesting things to look at and buy. Take your time along
Österlånggatan, Köpmangatan and Svartmangatan. These
streets house shops that offer artistic items rather than
the usual tourist fare.

IRIS HANTVERK
Västerlånggatan 24
https://www.iris
hantverk.se/

Iris Hantverk started as
a small brush manufac-
turing company in the
late 19th century, and
remains successful today.
Each design is unique to
their shop, and made by
vision-impaired craftspeo-
ple. They also offer other
home goods like blankets,
cutting boards, and linen
hand towels, using pri-
marily natural materials.

Courtesy of Iris Hantverk, Anna Kern,
photographer

SÓL
Köpmangatan 18

This is a small shop tucked away on a side street, steps away from the main square. All of the products are hand-made from Swedish crafters, many unique and one-of-a-kind. This is a good place to stop if you are interested in items made by the Sami people. If you are unable to make it north to Jokkmokk, you can be assured that the pieces you find here are authentic and good quality. The shop owners are interested in the history of the crafts they carry, and base much of their judgment on museum collections to evaluate the authenticity and character of the products they carry.

▲ *detail of the 13th century Skogbonaden tapestry*

➢ *Gold collar, 5th century Västergötland, Möne*

Bruce Nappi, photographer (top) Statens historiska museet, Wikimedia Commons (right)

Courtesy of Sól Handkraft

You will not be at a loss for finding a place to eat, but some favorites for lunch or fika (coffee break) are: Under Kastanjen (Kindstugatan 1), Mäster Olofsgården (Svartmangatan 6) or Grillska huset (Köpmangatan 15).

Central Stockholm

THE SWEDISH HISTORY MUSEUM
Naravägen 13-17
https://historiska.se/

This is a great place to start a trip through Central Stockholm (or to end your day with afternoon tea), particularly if you have an interest in the Vikings and Middle Ages. The galleries follow a chronology that helps the visitor to understand the evolution of Swedish civilization and culture from pre-historic times, and is told from the viewpoint of individuals whose excavated remains illustrate that society. A few garment fragments have been found that tell a great deal about textile technology. The hoards of silver and gold from Viking times are truly astonishing, and tell a wonderful story of the trade between the Middle East and Scandinavia.

HEMSLÖJDEN
Norrlandsgatan 20
https://hemslojden.org/

The shop for the National Association of Swedish Handcraft Societies carries Yllet Gotlandsgarn (Gotland + Falkland Is. *Merino* spun in Denmark), Ullgarn 6/2 and Lovikka yarn from Ullcentrum Öland, and Yarns & Barns *UllRika* (*Jämtland* wool) as well as linen from Växbo. They have wonderful weaving yarns as well, in addition to a wide range of handcrafts, books and home

SW photo

goods. Even though I can't easily translate the articles, I also find I need to pick up one or two issues of their gorgeous crafts magazine for inspiration.

On the way to Wincent Rowen, stop in at **Bengt & Lotta** (Norrtullsgatan 3, *http://www.bengt-lotta.se*) for more souvenir shopping Their small shop has wonderful socks with Nordic designs, and other handcrafts of their own design.

WINCENT ROWAN
Norrtullsgatan 27, 113 27 Stockholm, Sweden
http://wincentgarner.se/

This is a shop that feels like your own local yarn store; cozy and welcoming, where the major offering is Rowan yarn. They are the Rowan distributor in Stockholm. I also found other temptations from Germany and South Africa on my last visit, and they are also sourcing linen yarns (spun in Sweden) in the spring/summer season.

If you are feeling like a sweet treat, there is an excellent coffee shop (**Nybergs Konditori & Café**) next door with outstanding cookies and huge cups of tea.

South of Gamla Stan

LITET NYSTAN
Sankt Paulsgatan 20
https://www.litetnystan.se/

Even if you have no other places on your agenda for the area south of Gamla Stan, here is a shop you will want to visit that is a quick walk from the Mariatorget subway stop. Litet Nystan is packed with an international selection of yarn, from throughout Scandinavia, as well as the UK, Portugal, Switzerland, Germany, Estonia, and North and South America. For Swedish offerings they include the products of Kampes Wool Spinneri (New Zealand wool spun in Sweden) with z-ply yarns for two-end knitting, and Lovikka yarn. They also have Karin Öberg's linen (imported flax spun at Holma-Helsinglands), Yllet (Gotland wool + Faulklands merino spun in Denmark) and the locally sourced Östergötlands wool from Odeshog. Östergötlands yarn is featured in some of Ivar Asplund's designs. His excellent book *Sticka Flätor*, was released in English by Trafalgar Square Press in the fall of 2019. If you are lucky, you might find him in the shop helping customers or teaching a class. The entire staff is helpful and welcoming, so plan to spend some time looking through the yarn selections. There is a lot packed into a small space!

More to See in Stockholm

Find a way to work at least two of the many museums in Stockholm into your schedule. Top on the list should be

Sara and Karin at Winset Rowan, where the book idea was born

At Litet Nystan in the Mariatorget neighborhood

the outdoor museum Skansen and the Nordiska Museum. These two, along with historic buildings, the Vasa Museum (an intact 17th century ship that sank in 1628), and the ABBA Museum are located on Djurgården island (all easily accessible by bus and tram from central Stockholm).

A visit to **Skansen** (*https://www.skansen.se/*), an open-air museum and zoo, will provide you with a glimpse into pre-industrial Sweden in different parts of the country. In addition to houses displaying a variety of crafts in production, you will find animals from the wild and two flocks of heritage breed (endangered) sheep. It's easy to spend a full day there, capped off by a trip to the gift shop where you'll find many of the crafts for sale, as well as embroidery and knitting yarn, some weaving tools, and a good selection of books. There also are several places for lunch or fika, and often are musical performances during the summer. In late November and through December, the site is decorated for Christmas and outdoor market stands abound.

The **Nordic Museum** (Nordiska museet, *https://www.nordiskamuseet.se/*) features the history and ethnography of Sweden, including extensive textile exhibitions. Within those exhibits is a textile study area with slide-out drawers of dozens of textile techniques, available to peruse at your leisure. The museum also has an impressive library that holds monthly knit cafés with lectures on a variety of craft topics, as well as periodic knit meet-ups for new knitters. As with most museums, the museum shop is a great place to add to your collection of high-quality

⋏ *Nordiska museet*

Jordgubbe, photographer (above), Bruce Nappi, photographer (left)

souvenirs, books, and crafts. There also is a small café for lunch or fika, with fresh and interesting daily selections.

FINDING YARN IN UPPSALA

Just 44 miles north of Stockholm (and easily accessible by commuter rail), Uppsala is the oldest center of higher education in Scandinavia. The University was founded in 1477, and one of its renowned scholars, Carl Linnaeus lived and had his gardens there. Known as the "father of modern taxonomy," his trips across Sweden in the 1740s to find, document and classify plants and animals, contribute to our understanding of the interesting landscapes of Gotland and Öland Islands.

⋏ *Views of Skansen Open Air Museum*

Bruce Nappi and Sara Wolf, photographers

Gamla Uppsala (old Uppsala) was an important pagan center in Sweden, housing wooden idols of the Norse gods Odin, Thor and Freyr. While the pagan temples have long ago disappeared, some 250 burial barrows (of possibly 2-3,000 original graves) remain, with some thought to hold the remains of kings from the 5th and 6th centuries. It is an interesting site to visit, located on the north side of town and accessible by bus.

The **Uppsala Cathedral** (*svenskakyrkan.se/uppsala/ domkyrkan*), begun in the late 13th century is a "must" for knitters with an interest in the early history of knitting. The so-called *Sture glove*, one of the very limited number of early knitted garments with a known date (1547) is housed in the Cathedral's Treasury Museum (see page 13) along with other important textiles including the golden gown of Queen Margaret (1353–1412).

Uppsala Castle (*uppsalasmuseer.se/english/eng_ uppsala_slott.html*), dating to the 16th century, houses the Uppsala Art Museum, and its beautiful gardens are worth a visit as well. Depending on the time of year, you might

⌃ *Landscaping sheep at Uppsala Castle*

SW photo

run into the 4-footed landscapers who take care of the hillside behind the castle.

After wandering through all of these historic sites, as well as across the University grounds with lovely standing stones, the commercial center of Uppsala is nearby with the town's single yarn shop, and the **Upplands Museum**. Upplandsmuseet, S:t Eriks torg, *www.upplands museet.se*.

The museum has a small footprint in the city, but has multiple outreach and partnering programs that might have you planning your trip to coincide with a festival or wool market. The exhibits include both historical materials and changing galleries as well as a very good museum shop. You can find the calendar of events online.

Many museum programs take place at Gamla Uppsala, and in August, they used to help sponsor the Wool Market at Österbybruk, a 45-minute train ride from Uppsala Station. The market (now sponsored by local businesses) is a celebration of Swedish wool, and the event includes lectures, classes, demonstrations, and of course, vendors of fleece and yarn. It is billed as a family event, with a number of activities and games for children. The location is a lovely historic complex of buildings around a 17th century forge known for its central role in the development of the Swedish iron and metal industry.

YLL O TYLL
Bredgränd 7
https://www.yllotyll.com/

Yll o Tyll carries a range of Scandinavian yarns (Drops, Rauma Finullgarn and Sandes Garn from Norway; Hjelholts and Isager from Denmark and Léttlopi from Iceland). The

▲ Yarns of Yll o Tyll

Courtesy of Yll O Tyll

and fashion consumption. For example, their exhibit *Gothenburg's Wardrobe* (May 2019–August 2021) asked important questions about what fashion reveals about its time and what we can learn from a single piece of clothing. The museum also houses the very important 17th century waistcoat (see page 15) that ushered early sweater knitting into Sweden.

GÖTEBORGS REMFABRIK
Åvägem 15
http://remfabriken.se/en/

▲ Gotebörgs Remfabrik museum and ribbons trims made on their looms

Courtesy Föreningen Göteborgs Remfabrik, Katrin Bjerrome, photographer

two Swedish brands they carry are Yllet and Järbo. They also market their own brand of linen yarn, simply called *Lin*. It is a beautiful yarn that comes in deeply saturated colors that are difficult to capture in a photograph. Spun by Holma Hälsingland in Sweden, it sells quickly online and in the shop, with new colors each season.

FINDING YARN AROUND GOTHENBURG

The city of Gothenburg is a good place to begin a search of Sweden's west coast. In town are many museums, including two of special interest to crafters. There also are several yarn shops, and you are a short distance away from Udevalla and Borås as well as Öströö Fårfarm (for a visit to some *Gotland* sheep)

GÖTEBORGS STADSMUSEUM
Norra Hamngatan 12, 411 14 Göteborg
https://goteborgsstadsmuseum.se/en

This museum has an excellent historic clothing collection and frequent exhibits that deal with changing fashion

▲ The City Museum of Gothenburg is located in an 18th century house originally built for the Swedish East India Company

Ankara, own work

Here is a former textile mill founded in 1891, now run as a heritage museum by volunteers. When the mill closed in 1977, the city acquired the building and locals banded together to form the preservation society that maintains the machinery and handles visits from the public. Open only on the second Sunday of each month from 11–2 and Mondays from 5:30–7:30, their guided tours feature working textile machines including braiders and four bobbin lace machines from Barmen, Germany. You'll find ribbons and trims in the museum shop that volunteers have made on the looms, as well as books and postcards. The volunteers also train interns how to use the machinery to insure their management well into the future.

KNIT AND PURL

Bondegatan 7, 416 55 Göteborg

https://www.knitandpurl.se/

This small shop located not far from the train station features Sandnes yarn from Denmark and lovely patterns by Cecilie Skog and Tiril. They also carry a good selection of Addi needles and Clover notions.

DEISY DESIGN

Kungsportsavenyn 39, 411 36 Götebord

https://deisydesign.nu/

This shop on Kungsportsavenyen is a source for Drops yarns and Lana Grossa *Slow Wool*, a wool/linen blend. The company was started by Deisy Barnevik-Berglund in 1966 and initially focused on the sale of hand-knit garments. Now located in Gothenburg, the shop is run by Deisy's daughter, Linda. The shop still features their own designs for you to knit along with their continuing line of ready-to-wear.

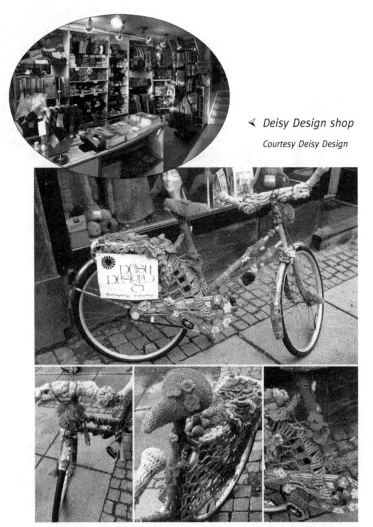

◁ *Deisy Design shop*

Courtesy Deisy Design

Nearby In Uddevalla

BOHUSLÄNS MUSEUM

Museigatan 1, Udevalla

https://www.bohuslansmuseum.se/en/

Uddevalla is about 55 miles north of Gothenburg. A trading port and hub for herring fishing, its location contributed to a political history where the region was traded back and forth between Sweden and Norway several times well into the 18th century. The museum, located in the center of town, features exhibitions about the history and natural history of the region. Learn about the maritime rock carvings from the middle ages and then visit them along the Bohus coastline.

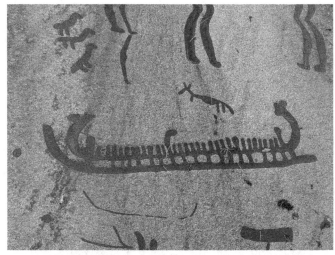

⌃ *Maritime rock carvings*

Public domain, Wikipedia commons

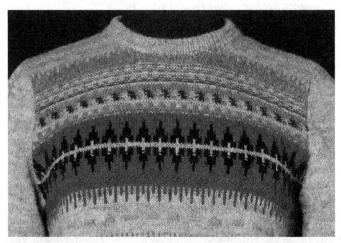

⌃ *Red Edge designed by Anna-Lisa Mannheimer Lunn, mid 1940s. Available as a knitting kit.*

Courtesy of Bohusläns Museum

You also will find a small exhibit on Bohus Stickning, and the museum shop carries the important publication, *Bohus Stickening: The Revival* by Viveka Overland, as well as kits for sweaters, hats and gloves. They provide for mail order and this is the only place where you will be able to buy the yarn and patterns for these historic designs in person.

Nearby In Borås

THE SWEDISH SCHOOL OF TEXTILES

Allégatan 1, Borås

https://www.hb.se/

The textile school in Borås was founded in 1866 as the Technical School of Weaving. With courses in management, materials technology and fashion, it is a hub of contemporary (and traditional) design with a vibrant international community of students and educators.

The Textile Museum is located at The Textile Fashion Center:

Skaraborgsvägan 3

https://textilmuseet.se/

With a costume collection featuring clothing from the 1870s to the 1920s in additional to traditional Swedish folk costume the Textile Museum is yet another treasure. They collect in the area of textile printing technology, including textile mill products and sample books. For children there is a "try on" collection—the ultimate in dress up for kids. Add to this a lovely café/restaurant, and you'll have a very pleasant visit.

Courtesy of Creative Commons, Annika Cross, photographer

South of Gothenburg

HALLAND MUSEUM OF CULTURAL HISTORY

Fästmomgem1, Varberg, Sweden

https://www.museumhalland.se/

Housed in the Varberg Fortress, the Halland Museum has the remains of the unique 14th century clothing of the "Bocksten Man" on display that served as inspiration for hand spinners competing in the 2019 championships. This exhibit and others give a good overview of medieval history in western Sweden in a 13th century fortification that also served as a prison. Their museum shop sells a variety of regional crafts and souvenirs and occasionally yarn from nearby hand dyers. There also is a very good café with a glass floor overlooking one of the archeological finds made during the renovation of the building; a medieval baking oven.

ÖSTRÖÖ FÅRFARM

Öströö Gård, Tvååker

https://www.ostroofarfarm.com/

Heading east from Varberg in beautiful countryside you can find yourself at the Öströö sheep farm where Kristian and Jeanette Carlsson have built a thriving, multi-faceted business from humble beginnings and 30 sheep. In addition to winning prizes for the outstanding food in their café, the Carlssons received the Sheep

⋀ *Halland Museum (top) and Öströö Fårfarm (bottom)*

Bruce Nappi and Sara Wolf, photographers

Entrepreneur of the Year Award in 2019 from the Svenska Fåravelsförbundet (the sheep trade association) in recognition of their promotion of sheep and wool products. The yarn and fleece in their shop (as well as all of the sheep-related crafts) come from their own sheep and are designed by Jeanette. If you arrive during the spring lambing season (April–May), you are invited to watch quietly in the sheep barn where between 900 and 1,000 lambs are born each year. As an interesting side note, the nearby town Tvååker means "flax fields," although none are found there these days.

FINDING YARN ON GOTLAND ISLAND

Gotland Island is, quite simply, a magical place. With Viking ruins, the remains of historic churches, a windswept landscape and *Gotland* sheep throughout the countryside, it is a wooly heaven. Even the traffic bollards are shaped like the local sheep.

The original name of the settlers of the island (Gutes) is the same name given to the native, and oldest breed of Swedish sheep (*Gutefår*). These people and their descendants not only developed a strong agricultural base, but also established the main city of Visby as a major trading port within the Baltic region. Ships came into Visby to trade, and Viking ships based there traveled to Great Britain, along the European coast and into the Mediterranean. Hoards of silver and gold coins found on Gotland include currency from all over Europe and the Muslim world.

⋏ Sankta Karin Church, Visby, constructed between 1235 and 1412 as the church of a Franciscan convent

SW photo

The rune stones on Gotland are unique. In addition to the characteristic interlaced designs, they often tell a story. There are wonderful examples in the museum in Visby as well as some that remain outside in the landscape.

While the rune stones tell part of the story of pre-Christian Gotland, more of the history can be found in the medieval churches across the island. Gotland has the highest concentration of medieval churches in northern Europe (98 in all), many of which retain parts of their original frescoes. Of these, ten lie within Visby's medieval city walls.

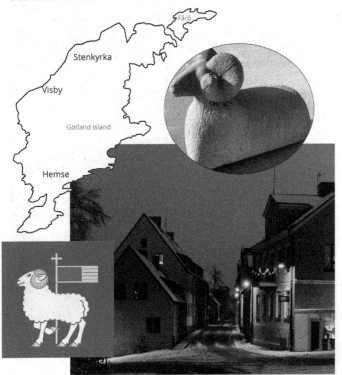

⋎ The snake-witch stone (left) and Stora Hammars stone (right) on Gotland Island

Berig, own work, Wikipedia Commons

Stenkyrka Ullspinneri

A range of yarn and home goods available in the Visby shop
SW photo

A Design and Hantverk and Stenkyrka Ullspinneri

Photos courtesy of Design and Hantverk and Sara Wolf

DESIGN AND HANTVERK, GOTLAND
S:t Hansgatan 30a, Visby
https://www.dhgh.se/

This shop carries 2- and 3-ply 100% *Gotland* yarn from their mill Stenkyrka Ullspinneri located in the north part of the island. They also have 2-ply, z-spun yarn, and locally sourced alpaca. The shop imports Icelandic wool and some other European brands, and is the distributor for Ashford on the island.

A The Yllet flagship store in Visby

SW photo

YLLET
S:t Hansgatan 19
http://www.yllet.se/

Yllet sells not only their yarn brand, kits and patterns, but a variety of wool clothing and home goods at their shop in Visby. While the bulk of their yarns are *Gotland* breed wool with a small percentage of Falkland Island *Merino* added for softness, they recently have been producing a 75% kid mohair and 25% Falklands *Merino* yarn in five natural shades.

The shop has a knowledgeable and helpful staff able not only to help with your knitting projects but also suggest ways in which to incorporate traditional Gotland designs into your own knitting. That is the idea behind Frida Asplund's sampler of patterns from *The Mitten Book*[1]—designs that originally came from the fragments collected by Hermanna Stengård in the early 20th century (see page 21).

Ullgarn Extra 2, with 27 color choices is perfect for color work, and is featured in many of their cardigan designs. One of their mitten or hat kits is a good introduction to knitting with their wool.

A Frida Asplund's Gotland design sampler

Bruce Nappi, photographer

RINGMURENS HEMSLÖJD
Adelsgatan 2, Visby
http://ringmurenshemslojd.com/

Ringmurens Hemslöjd is in a new site near the city walls (just around the corner from their original location). With an emphasis on handicrafts of all kinds, there is a good selection of Gotland-produced wool, particularly from artisans with limited, specialized production. It is

Ull Och Piano

⌃ Ull och Piano yarn is available only on Gotland Island.
Kirstin Blom's Blood Moon Shawl knit by Brenda Fillion using
two shades of Ull Och Piano yarn (right).

Sara Wolf and Lauren Nappi, photographers

one source for *Ull och Piano* spun and dyed at Ihre Gård Ullspinneri. They also carry a number of lovely hat and mitten patterns, including several featuring Hermanna Stengård's designs.

KVINNFOLKI HANTVERK GOTLAND
Donners Plats
https://www.kvinnfolki.se/

Near the Visby Harbor is a crafts cooperative of 16 Gotland women where one of the crafters is found in the shop each day. Featuring glass, ceramics, leather, textiles, woodworking, jewelry and artisan specialty foods, Kvinnfolki is likel to consume quite a bit of your time with its array of high quality offerings. Housed in a lovely historic building at Donners Plats, the shop is filled with light even on dark winter days, and has an air of exuberance and whimsy. There were both mill-spun and hand-spun (and dyed) yarns available in a variety of weights and styles, all from *Gotland* sheep and crafters, and like all artisanal products, these change often.

OTHER PLACES TO VISIT

GOTLANDS MUSEUM
(FÖRENINGEN GOTLANDS FORNVÄNNER)
Strandgatan 14
https://www.gotlandsmuseum.se/

The best introduction to prehistoric Gotland is found at the Gotlands Museum. In addition to an impressive collection of picture stones, the galleries show historic battles, including the battle against the invading Danes in 1361. Throughout the galleries are small vignettes focusing on the life of individual historic characters that give the viewer a window into the times and materials on display from a more personal point of view.

Some of the most impressive artifacts are the archeological collections recovered from Spillings farm. The so-called "Spillings Hoard" (Spillingsskatten) is the world's largest Viking silver treasure, of nearly 150 pounds of coins and other objects. Remnants of a lock lead scholars to believe that the caches may have been held in locked chests. Other artifacts like glass beads, tiles, iron nails, objects of bronze and copper and brick revealed that the site had been continuously occupied for over 1,000 years, up to the 19th century.

◄ Kvinnfolki at
Donners Plats

Courtesy of Kvinnfolki
Hantverk, Leena Jokela,
photographer

➤ Gotlands Museum

W. Carter, photographer

△ Treasures from the Gotlands Museum

SW photos

◁ Annika Ulbricht and Elin Wilson, apprentice spinners at Gotlands Spinneri with shop samples of patterns for their yarn

SW photo

With an abundant number of craft shops, design stores, coffee shops and restaurants, Visby has the feel of an artist colony. Many shops are closed during the winter, but stalwarts remain available with limited hours year-round. Some of note are:

- **Jordnära** (ecological cotton designer clothing)
- **Kränku** (tea and coffee)
- **Akantus** (interior design)
- **Ödins Garveri** (sheepskin clothing and furnishings)
- **Ett Rum För Resande Café** (best cup of coffee in Visby, right down the street from Yllet)

To the South

GOTLANDS SPINNERI
Fardhem Sandarve 712, Hemse
http://www.gotlandsspinneri.se/

Gotlands Spinneri is located south of Visby near the village of Hemse. Like many of these small mills, this factory has a specialty—spinning 100% *Gotland* breed wool. They have been at this for 30 years and the yarn is impeccable.

When asked about the rumored difficulty of spinning *Gotland* wool, the response (with a patient smile) was that they only knew how to spin *Gotland* wool, so they thought it was easy. Although the website only shows

wool in the natural colors of the sheep, the mill has begun to work with dyes to expand their range. They also are hoping to have a web shop operational in the near future. Meanwhile, you can email or call them to obtain their yarn and other products, or buy yarn right at the mill when you visit.

To the North

STENKYRKA ULLSPINNERI
Stenkyrka, Gard 176 Tingstäde
https://www.ullspinneri.se/

You will find the Stenkyrka Ullspinneri just outside the small village of Stenkyrka (which translates as Stone Church). This is a mini-mill that produces yarn for Design and Hantverk, featuring not only the local *Gotland* sheep, but yarns from local alpaca. Their small on-site shop also has some of the imported brands carried in Visby, but you might luck into finding something unusual as well. Since they do some lönspinning, there might be some skeins left from that production. I was lucky to find a skein of *Texel*—the only time I found yarn from that breed (except in blends).

THE BUNGEE MUSEET
Road 148, Fårösund
https://www.bungemuseet.se/

The Bunge Museet (open only in the summer) is another of the outdoor historic museums in Sweden not far from Fårösund and the Ferry to Fårö Island The buildings are thatched with *ag*, a marsh grass, and the museum shows three centuries of buildings and building construction. Some of the most famous of the Gotland prehistoric picture stones also have been relocated to the site.

⌄ *Bunge Museet grounds*

SW photo

⋀ *Landscape and Rauks at Langhammars, Fårö*

SW photo (top), Guillaume Baviere, Wikipedia Commons (bottom)

◁ *Prehistoric picture stone (left) and historic building construction (above)*

Courtesy of Wikimedia Commons, Wolfgang Sauber, photographer

Fårö Islands

If you have gotten as far as Stenkyrka, keep heading north and take the 15-minute ferry ride to Fårö Island. This small, windswept and remote island just off of Gotland in the Baltic Sea is known for its *rauk* formations, limestone from the Silurian period (443 million years ago) that has been eroded into fantastical shapes by the action of the waves.

Filmmaker Ingmar Bergman and his wife Ingrid von Rosen are buried in the cemetery of Fårö kyrka, the main church on the island, dating to the 14th century.

Bergman (1918–2007), Swedish director, writer and producer, called Fårö home, particularly in his later years. It now houses the Bergman Center and the summer Bergman film festival.

⋀ *Fårö kyrka, one of the many medieval churches in the Gotland area*

SW photo

More Gotland History

Because of its unique location in the Baltic, Gotland Island provided a trading port through which a significant number of goods and products moved. The island was well known for knitting both in other European ports and on the Swedish mainland. Swedes were also living in nearby Estonia as early as the 13th century, and between 1561 and 1721 Estonia was ruled by Sweden.

▲ 19th century knitters on Gotland Island

Courtesy of the Gotlands Museum

Inger and Ingrid Gottfridsson[1] recount the island knitting history as beginning in the 17th century. The best-known tales are of the so-called "sweaterhags," women who gathered knitted garments from households all over the island, and brought them to Visby yearly to sell. One sweaterhag would take as many as 800 sweaters to Stockholm, returning in time for the Christmas holidays.

The Baltic is rough and unpredictable, and on one such journey in the fall of 1824 the returning ship was blown off course and finally came onshore on the Estonian coast. After a month, the boat was able to reach Gotland on Christmas Eve, creating a wonderful celebration for the families who had thought their friends and relatives had died at sea.

There are many other connections between Estonia and Sweden. The earliest reference in Estonia to knitting is from 1664 when 115 pairs of knitted stockings were taken from western Estonia to Sweden.[2] Anu Pink also points out other parallels with Swedish stocking traditions, particularly there. In addition to shared commerce, Swedes living along the Estonian coast and introduced the red stockings worn widely in that region. The stockings are similar to some in the Nordiska Museet in Stockholm.[3]

There also is a reference in *Estonian Knitting 1: Traditions and Techniques* of a Swedish woman being hired in the 17th century to teach spinning on the estate of Claes Tott in Läänemaa County (Western Estonia). The teacher initially instructed 10 women, who then spread the skill to others.[4]

FINDING YARN ABOVE THE ARCTIC CIRCLE

The geographical designations for northern Sweden can be a little confusing. Norrbotten Province contains most of the area traditionally referred to as Lappland. The southern ⅓ of Lappland also is part of Västerbotten, so the political and geographical references don't quite match. Still, this is the region north of the Arctic Circle, and part of the traditional homeland to the Sami people.

Tsuguliev, Shutterstock.com

The earliest knitting publication I was able to find about Norrbotten province is Marika Larsson's book, *Stickat från Norrbotten: Vantar, sockor och Mössor* from 1978.[5] Other publications featuring northern Swedish and Sami design iclude: Soleig Larsson's *Knitting Mittens*,[6] and *Discover the Wonderful World of Sami Knitting*, by Laura Ricketts.[7] A deep dive into the history of northern mittens with pages of beautiful illustrations for inspiration is Erika Bordvall Falck's *Fancy Mittens*.[8]

There is a phenomenal collection of clothing at Ájtte (The Swedish Mountain and Sami Museum) in Jokkmokk, where the museum shop sells kits for locally designed mittens. If your travels take you there, the landscape is renown for hiking and fishing in summer, and of course, the northern lights and dog (or reindeer) sledding in winter. You can spend a night in the ice hotel, or if you are lucky enough to find accommodations, visit the Winter Market, beginning the first Thursday in February each year (as it has been since 1605).

The Market began as an important gathering and opportunity for trading among the indigenous Sami and other northern peoples around the Arctic Circle.

https://www.jokkmokksmarknad.se/en/

⋀ Take note of the lovely mittens in these photos.

Paolo Airenti, Shutterstock.com (left) and Shutterstock.com (right)

⋀ Winter Market in Jokkmokk

Courtesy of Wikimedia Commons

While knitted garments are secondary to items made of reindeer skin in this region, knitted hats, mittens and scarves have been common among the Sami from at least the 17th century. This is documented in the book *Lapponia*, by Johannes Schefferus (1673) who described knitting with fine iron needles and sheep and/or rabbit wool.[9]

Excavations (1907 and 1947) at the Jukkasjärvi church built over a burial ground beginning in about 1606 turned up many coffins as well as mummified remains that included a significant amount of knitted clothing (see page 23).

An interesting aspect of some of the patterns found on northern mittens and gloves are their presence all across the settlements and areas inhabited by the Sami people in Sweden, Finland (part of Sweden until 1809), Norway, and even into Russia. Although there are designs that are associated with specific villages or areas, the so-called *Norwegian Star* is the type of pattern found throughout the region, and is a reflection on the fact that these are from a nomadic people rather than patterns that have an origin in a specific place.

Another pattern type found throughout the area (and also documented in Gotland) is näversäcksbinding (entrelac in English).[10]

Jukkasjärvi Church

Courtesy of Wikimedia Commons, htm, photographer

Norwegian Star pattern

Courtesy of Creative Commons, Nils R Barth, photographer

Swedish wickerwork

Shutterstock.com

Lady with wickerwork backpack knitting mitten or sock in the round

Courtesy of the Nordiska museet (NMA.0070030), Karolina Kristensson, photographer.

Näversäcksbinding fragment

Courtesy of Erika Falck, Kasja Tuolja, photographer

This technique also shows up in early 19th century in Germany and Estonia, but its origins are unknown. It is possible that the designs may have come from one of the widely distributed pattern books circulating out of Germany at that time. There are a number of older examples of knee-high socks worked in this technique.

Simple stranded diamonds (also known as "faux entrelac") resembling näversäcksbinding also are often found on Sami mittens.

⋏ *Sami mittens in faux entrelac*

Courtesy of Nordiska museet (NM.015469A-B), Monika Djerf, photographer

Shopping in Jokkmokk

Hantverksbutiken (Porjusvägan 10, Jokkmokk) is not only a handicrafts shop in Jokkmokk, but also a place to purchase yarn to try the näversäcksbinding or the faux entrelac designs for mittens.

Stoorstålka (Föreningsgatan 2, Jokkmokk) carries yarn and mitten kits designed by Erika Nordvall Falck, featuring Siessá and Áhkko yarns. They also carry a range of cone yarns for band weaving as well as beginner kits to get started on Sami designs for band weaving.

Ájtte museum shop (Kyrkogatan 3) also carries mitten kits with both Erika Falck and Laura Ricketts Sami mitten projects.

Perhaps the most famous mittens from the north come from Lovikka. They were created by Erika Aittamaa in 1892 and if you don't have an urge to make them yourself, you'll find them in craft shops all across the north.

Making mittens remains an important activity for folks in the north of Sweden. The variety in local patterns, as well as designs that are shared across the area

⋏ *Lovikka mittens*

Shutterstock.com

around the Arctic Circle are plentiful and endlessly interesting to knit. Their importance was evident in 2019 at the Vantfestival in Junosuando, where 140 pairs of mittens borrowed from Estonia, Latvia, the Faroe Islands, Norway, Finland, Greenland, Iceland, Åland and Sweden. One of the exhibition organizers, Monika Lund, is publishing a book based on the exhibition. Photographs of the exhibition and prize-winning mittens can be found at her website, *http://vantarinorden.com*. Under the section "Vantgalleri" are photographs of many of the mittens from the exhibit, and a pattern for an Åland style mitten with thrums.

FOOTNOTES

1. Gottfridsson, Inger and Ingrid Gottfridsson, *The Mitten Book.* 1987, Asheville, NC, Lark Books, 1984.

2. Pink, Reimann and Jöste, *Estonian Knitting 1*, 2016, Türi, Saara Publishing House. P8.

3. Pink, Anu. *Estonian Knitting 2: Socks and Stockings.* 2018, Türi, Saara Publishing House, p. 90-91.

4. Pink, Reimann and Jöste, *Estonian Knitting 1*, 2016, Türi, Saara Publishing House, page 90.

5. Larsson, Marika. *Stickat från Norrbotton.* Stockholm, LTs förlag, 1978.

6. Larsson, Solveig, *Knitted Mittens.* North Pomfret, VT, Trafalger Square Books, 2015.

7. Ricketts, Laura. *Discover the Wonderful World of Sami Knitting: 5 Mitten Patterns from Finland, Norway & Sweden to Knit.* An eBook from *PieceWork* Magazine, www.needleworktraditions.com, n.d.

8. Falck, Erika Nordvall. Fancy Mittens—Markkinavanthuit. Jokkmokk, Sweden, Ájtte, Svenskt fjäll—och samemuseum, 2018.

9. Falck, Erika Nordvall. *Fancy Mittens.* Ájtte, p 8.

10. Other names for this in Swedish are: näverstickning, and näverkontstickning, referring to the birch bark baskets woven in this diamond-shaped design.

5 Spinning Mills, Sheep Farms, Artisans, and Their Products

There is a broad spectrum of spinning mills, large and small, across Sweden. They range from large, family run, multi-generational businesses to small start-ups with only one or two employees. They also vary widely in the types of products they offer, from single-breed fleece and yarn, to mixed breed, all-Swedish wool, and those that have all or part of the fleece imported. Some of these businesses are located at farms where their own animals form the basis of their products; other farms that welcome visitors send their fleece to mills and then sell the result in on-site shops. In addition to sheep wool, some mills also are processing alpaca, angora rabbit, and angora goat fleece. A few yarn companies send their fleece abroad for processing.

A feature of many spinning mills (and particularly smaller ones) is an emphasis on offering *lönspinning* services. This is a system where individual shepherds bring their fleece for processing either paying outright for the finished product they will sell elsewhere, or sharing the product with the mill for sale. There are many different business models for lönspinning, with the result that it often isn't completely clear to the buyer how a yarn was produced or its exact content. Many small yarn producers purchase fleece and have their special yarns made in these spinning mills for sale in venues like festivals and in online shops. With a little research, it is possible to find a number of artists who have unique and interesting yarns available. As with other small, or boutique businesses, however, these should be viewed as one-time offerings that may not be exactly duplicated again. This is part of the business of Swedish yarn that is very compelling and unique, but also frustrating if you hope to repeat a purchase.

In this chapter we will endeavor to list what various mills and farms have to offer, along with the best way to acquire their products. Many firms, including some of the larger ones, sell only from knitting shops in Sweden and elsewhere, and some with online stores ship only in Sweden. As with knitting shops, mills come and go, and their business model may change in time. We will endeavor to keep real-time updates on the website to reflect changes as we find them: *aknitwizard.com*.

Something to understand about Swedish yarns is their classification, quite different than the "sport," "fingering" and "worsted weight" that are typical in the US. Swedish yarns are classified by ply and weight/length. In other words, the Ullcentrum 2-ply wool that comes in 100-gram skeins with 300 meters/100 grams, is the equivalent of a light sport-weight yarn. It is helpful to use the WPI number if you plan on adapting these yarns to a pattern listing yarn weight as "sport" or "bulky."

WPI-Yarn Weight		
US Craft Council Designation	**Yarn Weight**	**Wraps/Inch**
0	Lace	›35
1	Fingering	19-22
2	Sport	15-18
3	DK	14-14
4	Worsted	9-11
5	Bulky	7-8
6	Super bulky	‹6

⌃ *Twist and Check*
Courtesy of Patrik Söderman

➢ *Stornoway Throw*
Courtesy of KnitPicks

For some of the older examples I documented in museum collections, the yarns didn't match any of the commercial examples available now. Some of these mittens were knit on very fine needles using a heavier yarn than is usual for that needle size. A good example is the *Gotland* mittens (see page 132) knit with Kampes 2-ply (heavy sport/light DK) on size 0 (2.0mm) needles. The yarn size I used was very similar to that of the original, but it probably would have taken my working on a 00 or even 000 to achieve the fineness of the original knitter's work.

Anita Yarn

https://www.etsy.com/shop/AnitaYarn

Anita Grahn is located in Uppsala, but her shop is virtual as well as frequently found at fairs and festivals. She takes advantage of many of the surrounding mini-mills, personally sourcing wool from a large variety of different Swedish breeds and her own angora rabbits. Her shop is one of the few where I found a consistent supply of bulky

lambs wool in addition to an ever-changing selection of fiber and fiber mixes.

Anita is also a very talented designer. Take a look at her Stornoway Throw and Twist and Check sock pattern.

Knitting with Anita's Yarn

I was lucky enough to meet up with Anita at the wool festival in Kil and have the opportunity to cuddle with her amazing yarns. I found myself with an impossible decision, and finally asked her to choose her favorites for me to "test drive."

I started with the *Finull*/angora blend (Fiberfröjd) which may have ruined me for future yarn choices. The angora is from her own bunnies, and she chose to blend it with the softest of baby *Finull* lamb. It's so soft it gave me shivers! What I really like best about it is that there is just enough of the angora to create softness, but not so much that you get that fuzzy angora look that makes you look like you have an aura around you. This is a very special yarn, and I'm looking forward to trying the others.

⌃ *Anita with her design* Snowdrops Shawl *in Semia yarn available on her Etsy site.*

Courtesy of Anita Grahn

⌃ *Some of Anita Grahn's yarn (left) and a swatch of Fiberfröjd (right)*
SW photos

Ateljé Lammet

http://www.ateljelammet.se/

I found Karin Skogh's *Finull* yarn at the Fårfest in Kil. She offers undyed brown wool from her own sheep in both singles and plied yarns. In addition to yarn, Karin holds sewing courses and makes traditional folk costume and dancing shoes. Her products are available online. Contact her via email from her website.

Knitting with Ateljé Lammet Yarn

I chose the singles yarn from Karin's farm for my test knit. At 20 wpi, this is a typical diameter for a fingering weight yarn, and might work well for a light and airy shawl. I found the spin to be slightly uneven, although not so obvious that it would show on a finished garment (see swatch). The stitches did fuzz up a little as I worked, making it likely that a lace project would be the best idea. In fact, I'm thinking that because the skein is quite large (just over 100g and 435 yards) I might make a 2-ply from the singles and use it for a cowl. *Finull* is very soft, and is great next to the skin.

◁ Finull *from Ateljé Lammet*

SW photos

⋏ Outside Båvains Spinhaus

SW photo

Båvens Spinhus

Båvens Spinnhus AB
Östra Industriområdet 3
649 30 Sparrenholm
https://www.bavensspinnhus.se/

Båvens is one of the best-known mini mills in Sweden. The bulk of their processing has come through lönspinning, but they also produce yarn for many small crafters as well as for sale in their own shop. Their products, coming solely from Swedish breeds, do vary somewhat from time to time depending on the fibers brought to the mill for spinning. They produce z-plied yarns that are tightly spun and good to work with for tvåändsstickning. You might find alpaca in their shop as well. At present the shop sells only onsite, at wool fairs, and online in Sweden.

Recently Båvens has been working with the renowned dye artist Tante Kofte to produce beautiful, jewel-toned sock yarn of angora and wool. While the yarn may

⋏ *A selection of yarns spun by Båvens Spinhus and dyed by Tante Kofte*

SW photo

93

△ Åsa Nordqvist explaining the workings of some of the spinning machinery at Båvens Spinhus.

SW photo

initially feel too soft to make good socks, it is very tightly spun and is quite strong. You won't find "super wash" yarns here, so the recipient of a pair of socks made from Båvens wool must be "knit worthy," (and understand the importance of careful hand washing).

In addition to yarn, the mill offers knitting kits, felt products, and skins. They also hold courses in a variety of techniques and knitting cafés throughout the year, and can give you a tour of the mill by special request.

Knitting with Båvens Spinhus Yarns

I've been lucky to have several of the Båvens yarns to test and enjoy. Their z-ply for two-end knitting is very good quality, but limited only to the natural wool colors. I also enjoyed working with their *Dälapäls/Finull* blend. I already knew from working with the *Dälapäls* spun by Josefin that a yarn including the whole fleece would have good shine, but would not be completely soft. The addition of the *Finull* then, really makes a difference. Still, it has a bit of a rustic feel. What I really liked about it, however, was the clear stitch definition even with a fair amount of halo in the yarn. This yarn would work well for lace or cables as well as other textured stitches. That will be the

△ Swatch from Båvens blended wool

SW photo

subject of some future swatching, as meanwhile I've only just finished a stockinette example.

Borgs Vävgarner

Ängdalvägen 9A
Hässelholm
http://www.borgsvavgarner.se/

Established in 1734 in the town of Lund, Borgs Vävgarner was eventually bought by Glimåkra (famous for their looms) and by Bengt Holmqvist in 2000. Now located in Vittsjö in the south of Sweden, this small company sells both a wide range of linen weaving yarns and wool knitting yarn, as well as weaving tools. While they currently sell to individuals online only in Sweden and the UK, weaving stores internationally carry their products.

Filtmakeriet

Hallen 2813
823 91 Kilafors
https://filtmakeriet.se/om-filtmakeriet

Located in Kilafors (about 160 miles north of Stockholm), Filtmakeriet offers unspun wool (pre-yarn), and 2 and 3-ply yarns of mixed breed fibers; all in natural wool colors and dyed wools. They also offer both carded bats, and washed fleece of *Finull*, *Gotland*, *Leicester*, *Rya*, *Texel* and a *Helsinge/Gestrike* mix. They are one of the very few places in Sweden to obtain linen for spinning.

Run by two sisters, the mill works with the raw fleece through the preparation process to the finished products ranging from quilt wadding and upholstery material to felt, fleece for needle felting, and woolen yarn. They have limited open hours in the factory shop, and an online shop, but only ship within Sweden.

Filtmakeriet offers a number of courses. One of the most intensive is a 6-day class that occurs over a period of three months (with a significant amount of homework) that takes the student through basic knowledge of the different Swedish sheep and wool and how to prepare the fleece. The course works through all steps of the preparation process from sorting and washing, to the finished product. They cover not only yarn, but also needle felt and weaving.

Their website is interesting to visit, with good information about native breeds as well as their robust training program. Here is a note from the website that reflects their business philosophy: "by using more wool and less synthetic material, everyone can influence their own textile use in a way that protects the climate, our nature and culture." Filtmakeriet is a company that has a strong appreciation for the preservation of small business. They work directly with individual farmers and customers to increase the use of Swedish wool in a personal and sustainable way.

Knitting with Filtmakeriet Yarns

I test knit two yarns from Filtmakeriet; the yarn called "Hanny" (a mix of *Gotland*, *Texel* and *Svea*) and their dyed yarn called "Tweed".

Both yarns are of exceptional quality, well-spun, even, and very easy to work with. These are yarns made for hand knitters who want to have an assurance of a reliable yarn that should wear very well.

The blush-pink "Hanny" is quite a bit softer than most of the yarns I've knit that contain *Gotland* as a substantial proportion of the mix. In fact, I think it could be worn next to the skin unless you are particularly sensitive. It's pale color is accented by the dark shade of the *Gotland*, giving it visual as well as sensory texture. Even though it is available only in the one color, it would make a gorgeous sweater.

Every shade of the "Tweed," (available in both singles and 2-ply) are lovely, saturated colors, but I chose the dark blue because it had a slightly mottled look that reminds me of yarns made from recycled jeans material. This blend of *Finull*, *Svea*, *Gotland* and *Leicester* is a masterful selection of fiber that is both soft and lightweight. The *Gotland* is not easily discernable to the touch, but the yarn is stronger because of its addition. This is a workhorse of a yarn that I can see using over and over. The wonderful colors would be outstanding for colorwork.

This yarn is only available by mail order or at the mill shop in Sweden. If you are planning a trip, see if you can find a way to get some while you are there. It will be worth the effort.

Framgården

The first skein of Framgården I was given came from crafts fair at Österbybruk near Uppsala, and while it's a lovely *Värmsland* wool that is cocoa in color, I wanted to expand my possibilities for making something to include color. The dyeing came out well, with half of the yarn in deep red. My mistake was in not controlling the color to obtain more contrast in the shades, so the result looks a little muddy. That does not reflect at all on the yarn, which is lovely and was a good choice for a hat. It is a strong and robust yarn that can take quite a bit of abuse (I did quite a bit of ripping on this project because I got the count wrong more than once). Even after reknitting twice, the yarn didn't appear to have any compression or damage. I got a second skein at the Fårfest in Kil,

⋏ *Hanny (left) and Tweed (right) swatches from Filtmakeriet Yarns*

SW photos

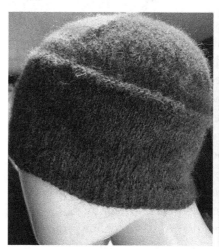

⋏ *Framgården* Värmsland *natural brown and hat project*

SW photos

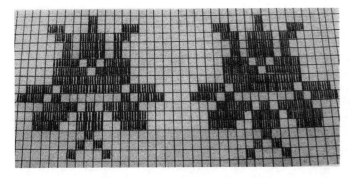

A Hermanna Stengård's chart for "Granny's Nightcap."

SW photos

A Hat knit with Gotlands Spinneri yarns

Leah Nappi, model; Lauren Nappi, photographer

and will make a second run at this design. The chart comes from Hermanna Stengård's *Gotländsk Sticksöm* (Akleja—European Columbine, also known as Granny's Nightcap). Now that I know the name of the flower, I plan to use it again, hopefully with a more appropriate blue or purple color.

Gotlans Spinneri
Fardhem Sandarve 712
612 52 Hemse
http://www.gotlandsspinneri.se/

Gotlands Spinneri has been producing 100% *Gotland* yarn for more than 30 years. Located south of Visby near the village of Hemse on Gotland Island, this small mill has developed a reputation for the consistent production of high-quality yarn. Traditionally they have not mixed their fleece with other breeds, but they are anticipating many changes in the near

SW photo

future. The original owners have hired 3 interns to learn the craft as well as both the mechanical and business components of the Spinneri. Over the next three years the owners hope to transition out of the business as their interns become master spinners with the aid of the Craft and Education Foundation. The Foundation's roots are in the 14th century where tailors were the first craftspersons to earn the right to the title of Master. By providing

low-interest loans both for the educational component and the opportunity for the students to purchase existing or begin new businesses, the Foundation in cooperation with the Swedish Craft Council is pairing students with mentors in many fields as diverse as breweries, farriers, bookbinders, weavers, and spinners.

Knitting with Gotland Spinneri Yarns

I used the pale grey *Gotland* lamb 2-ply and a mini-skein of the dyed *Gotland* yarn for the hat *Granny's Nightcap*. The *Gotland* lamb turned out to be quite a bit softer than many of the other yarns I've tried from that breed. Still, it's a little more rustic than many would like, and has a very obvious halo. Something appears to happen in the dyeing process, and the dyed skeins have many fewer of the scratchy outercoat hairs protruding from the yarn. They either are lost in the dye bath, or compacted within the twist. That was helpful in that the stranding for the hat fell across the forehead and didn't seem bother the hat model.

What I liked about these yarns was the absolutely wonderful consistency throughout the skein, something that hasn't always been the case with others of the mini-mills. The 30+ years this mill has been operating has given the spinners the opportunity to completely perfect their craft and produce a wonderful, 100% *Gotland* yarn.

Holma-Helsinglands

Linvägen 8, Forsa

https://www.holma.se/shop

Bockens Garner is a brand of linen yarns that is very well-known in Sweden and around the world. The Holma-Helsinglands mill that produces these linen and wool yarns has been in operation since 1898, and while they no longer do their own spinning, they do bleach, dye and prepare yarns for their customers. They are the source of many of the linen yarns you will find in Swedish yarn shops (they often produce limited editions specifically for individual shops, such as Yll O Tyll in Uppsala). The mill is a wholesaler, but individual customers can buy from their factory shop.

Knitting with Holma-Helsinglands Linen

The raspberry-colored linen yarn at Yll O Tyll drew me like a magnet. In fact, the various colors were so saturated and glossy that after standing and staring for a while, I had to revert to my standard method of choosing when I'm overwhelmed—go with the first one that got your attention. The shop had a lovely sample of a simple pullover worked in a very open lace pattern to wear over a camisole, and I immediately had about 50 ideas for stitches I thought would work for that kind of garment.

Working with linen does require patience (something I have in short supply), and the first thing that happened when I tried to wind it too quickly was that it slipped off the swift and landed in a huge tangle at my feet. It then spent weeks in "time out" until I could face the knots. I tried a number of stitch patterns, and still haven't found one I'm completely happy with. Let's just say I really admire folks who find linen an easy fiber to work with, and I haven't yet produced a swatch that I'm ready to share.

Höner och Eir

https://honer-och-eir.myshopify.com/

Caroline Henkelius and Knut Svensson are the owners and operators of Höner och Eir (formerly known as Zäta Spinneri) in Skaraborg. Unique features of this spinning mill are their limited edition runs of unspun singles that are hand-blended and hand-dyed wools from a variety of local sheep. They sell online only and their yarns are available for overseas shipments. Both their website and Caroline's Instagram page are full of gorgeous images of their Nutiden yarn, their own sheep, their wool-related tools (such as nålbinding needles), ceramics, and other

Courtesy of Höner och Eir

unique and ever-changing products. Each offering sells out quickly, so you may benefit from becoming a patron to receive notices of new products. The mill currently is unable to offer tours.

Knitting with Nutiden

My introduction to Nutiden came directly from Caroline Henkelius, who brought several cakes of the unspun pre-yarn for me to fondle as we spoke about her spinning mill and plans. I found it both exciting and intimidating. If you are knitting with a single strand, it requires a bit of skill to handle it properly. A quick tug can cause the fibers to separate and come apart. Happily, they also can be easily put back together, although using the traditional "spit splice" causes the fibers to bunch together and become matted. I found that just a little friction of rubbing between the fingers puts the strand together again.

Ʌ *Swatch knit from Nutiden (unspun singles).*

SW photo

Courtesy of Höner och Eir

Photos courtesy of Katrina Karlsson, Jacob Gården

A swatch of the single is as light as air, and would make a feather-soft shawl. Holding two strands together gives sufficient strength to make a sweater. Because of the amount of air in and around the fibers, it will also make a garment that is extremely warm. There are some stunning examples of shawls, sweaters and mitts made from Nutiden both on Ravelry, and within Caroline's Instagram pages. As some of the knitters have noted, you don't knit quickly with this yarn. It is a great one for so-called "mindful" knitting.

Jakob Gården

https://www.visitoverkalix.se/jakobgarden/

Above the Arctic Circle is a sheep farm along Lake Djupträsket (east of Jokkmokk and near the border with Finland) where you not only can find beautiful *Finull* lamb wool, but rent a cottage and spend time surveying the Norrbotten landscape.

Katarina Karlsson has been raising sheep and working with the silky-soft fleece of Swedish *Finull* for many years. She is a member of the Swedish Sheep Breeding and Swedish Finulls Association. Her Jakob Gården yarns (spun by Båvens Spinhus) are available at festivals like the annual Fårfest in Kil and the Crafts Market in Bränna, Överkalix. The yarn comes in 2- and 3-ply skeins, as well as a 4-ply (Midwinter Finull) with a slightly harder twist, available in cones.

Knitting with Jakob Gården Yarn

After knitting a few rows, the word that came to mind was "luscious." This is *Finull* at its best; smooth, buttery

⋀ *Överkalix, Norrbotten Province*

Courtesy of Wikimedia Commons. Mestos, photographer

⋀ *Swatch of 2-ply Jakob Gården Finull yarn*

SW photo

soft, and perfect next to the skin. The 2-ply is right at the edge of Sport and DK in weight (14-15 wpi). Depending on your personal tension, you probably could work on a US #4 or 5 needle without issues. I happened to like the rather dense feel on a smaller needle for something like a scarf or cowl. I'd likely go up a size (or two) for a sweater.

Järbo

The Järbo name is well known through Scandinavia, and the company produces a wide variety of yarns and offers dozens and dozens of free patterns. Their 100% wool is easy to work with, and predictable. If you are the least bit concerned about being able to choose a yarn that will work perfectly with their patterns, their own is a safe choice. The sizing of the yarn is consistent, and fits within the parameters of the Yarn Craft Council's standards. They offer many blended yarns (like llama and silk or alpaca and cotton), as well as novelty yarns, recycled fiber yarns and Icelandic wool. They are a wholesale-only company, but many shops with online boutiques carry this brand.

Kampes Spinneriprodukt AB

Ullervad, 542 93 Mariestad
http://www.kampes.se

Hjalmar Kampe founded Tidans Ullspinneri AB in 1891. This family company was renamed Kampes Spinneriprodukt AB in 1978 and continues to produce yarn to the present. Its products can be found in most knitting shops around Sweden, and include several weights of knitting yarns as well as z-ply yarns for two-end knitting, and bulky yarn for Lovikka mittens. While their yarn is produced in Sweden, the wool itself is actually *Merino* imported from New Zealand. Their yarns, as well as other imported yarns and knitting tools are available in their onsite boutique, open Monday-Friday 10-5 and by mail order within Sweden.

Knitting with Kampes Yarns

Since these yarns are found in so many yarn shops around Sweden (and are very popular among Swedish

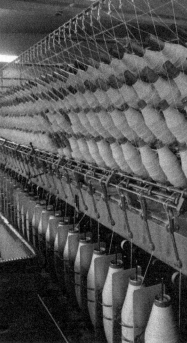

Inside the Kampes Spinning Mill
SW photo

knitters) I thought it would be a good idea to do some knitting with this brand to test its performance. Right off the top it needs to be said that this is a good, practical yarn with excellent consistency and a wide range of colors. It is also most recognizable in shops because it does not have a skein band for identification, and I have never seen a dye-lot differentiation. With that in mind, make sure to ask for help with your purchase, not only to get enough for your project but also to make sure that the skeins match.

I chose to knit the Gotland design Sun Wheel mittens (page 132) with Kampes wool for two reasons: first, the weight of the yarn knit at a fine gauge most closely resembled the original mitten from the swatches of various yarns I tried, and second, the colors were a decent approximation of the original for a dyed rather than natural brown and cream. I also felt like its wide availability made it particularly important to include in this review. One skein of each color was sufficient for these mittens, making it a very reasonable cost.

This was not an easy knit. I was working on US 0 (2.0mm) needles, and the yarn is about a DK weight (13 WPI). My first attempt was on double-points, but I switched to 2 circulars for this pattern because it was easier to control the join between needles. Also, the pattern is symmetrical, making it easier to see and "read" as I knit. There was quite a difference between the natural color and the dyed brown yarn. The natural (undyed) was rounder in profile, and the stitches were strongly defined. The brown seemed almost damaged in the dyeing process. It was matted and fuzzy in some places, thin in spots, and splitty in others. I found it difficult to work with, and some of the stitches got buried next to the more robust natural-colored stitches. In spite of the difficulties, the final product looks very nice, and I'm satisfied with the outcome. In the future I might use this yarn again because of its wide availability, but if I chose another dark color, I'd check the skein carefully to insure that the yarn appeared more robust and had a better profile to create even stitches.

Kampes is another of the mills in Sweden producing z-ply yarns for two-end knitting. This was one of the yarns I used when I took a course in tvåändsstickning from Karin Kahnlund at Sätergläntan Institute. During the course I had the opportunity to work with Båvens Spinhus and Wålstedts z-ply yarns to have a good comparison. I did enjoy working with all of the brands, and each has their own advantages. The Kampes wool was easiest on the hands (softest) but also is the most loosely plied. The Båvens z-ply is available in several fiber combinations, but its

Ꝉ *Mini-mitten in two-end technique using Kampes z-ply yarns*

SW photo

disadvantage is the limited range of colors. The skein I used contained some *Rya* fiber, making it exceptionally strong and robust. The brand I preferred was Wålstedts, with a very tight, hard spin and ply (as well as a good selection of colors). The profile of that yarn is also very round, and it handles well for the technique, sliding easily through your fingers. In truth, these differences are really minimal, and I'd recommend any of them for your projects. It all comes down to availability when you're in the market to buy.

Karlsbergsgården Spinneri

https://karlsbergsgarden.com/

This mill in Billebbarga processes angora rabbit, wool, mohair and alpaca for wool producers. They sometimes have yarn for sale at the mill, but their business is primarily production (lönspinning), not sales. This spinning mill prepares the yarns for Öströö Fårfarm (see knitting review below), and has spun yarn for Swedish Fibre. It is another small operation, but with great potential. The yarns I've handled so far are of good quality. Since they do not have a specific outlet, but rather act as a service business, you may not see their name directly associated with the yarn products you purchase.

Öströö Fårfarm

https://www.ostroofarfarm.com/

Located about 1 hour south of Gothenburg in the middle of the Åkulla beech forests and down a country lane, you'll find Öströö Fårfarm. Jeanette Carlsson and her husband began with a small farm and a small herd of *Gotland* sheep that has grown rapidly to become a thriving multi-faceted enterprise not only providing meat and wool to the community, but also serving as a conference

Ꝉ Gotland *lamb*

Courtesy of Öströö Fårfarm

⅄ *Some of the yarns offered in the Öströö Fårfarm shop*
Courtesy of Öströö Fårfarm

⅄ *Öströö 2-ply swatch*
SW photo

center and tourist destination. They have held wool festivals, and in 2019 served as the location and co-sponsor for the Swedish fleece and spinning championships. They provide tours of the farm, and during the spring invite visitors to meet and interact with their new lambs (about 900/year).

The large retail (and online) shop at the farm has a wonderful variety of crafts related to or made from sheepskins and wool (all designed by Jeanette). In addition, they offer a variety of yarns from their sheep (all in the natural colors of the fleece) that include both *Gotland* and a few *Leicester* for white wool. At times they also carry some dyed wool and fleece from both Kampes and Ullcentrum.

Öströö Fårfarm is a very family-friendly operation that has a wonderful small restaurant (with the best Chokladboller sweets I found in all of Sweden). You can sample their meat products on the menu, and also purchase them in their shop. The farm runs their own slaughterhouse (which you also can visit), so you know precisely where their products originate.

Knitting with Öströö Fårfarm Yarns

The farm has their fleece spun at Karlsbergsgården Spinneri, and as mentioned above, it is well spun and very consistent. I knit a swatch from the darker grey 3-ply *Gotland* yarn and loved the fabric it produces. It is a rustic yarn and the dense, long fibers in the mix give it a slight halo. Most people wouldn't want to wear this yarn next to the skin, but its springy texture and strength would make it an excellent choice for jackets or sweaters worn over another garment.

The yarn has a lovely sheen, and the tight spin is the basis for excellent stitch definition. This is quite different than the *Gotland* from Yllet that has a very pronounced

halo that obscures stitch definition. Öströö yarns also are recommended for felting, and felt quite easily.

I also swatched the light grey 2-ply. Since it is quite fine (19 wpi) I immediately thought of it as a lace-weight sample and decided to add some eyelets. It might be nice for a lightweight but very warm shawl. As it happened, I was working with it on a hot and humid day, and it felt uncomfortable in my hands, but after blocking, it relaxed quite a bit and the fibers seemed to stick out a little less. This particular skein has more than one color present, so is a lovely tweed, but much less regular than what I think of as a "tweed yarn." It's quite lovely, and the *Gotland* sheen is very evident.

Östergötlands Ullspinneri

info@ullspinneriet.se

Ulla-Karin Hellsten and Börje Norberg have been operating their mill for the past 35 years as part of the Östgötatextil regional network of independent textile

⅄ *Ulla-Karin Hellsten and Börje Norberg at Östergötlands Ullspinneri*
Courtesy of Östergötlands Ullspinneri

⌃ Connected Shirt by Katarina Brieditis

⌃ Freja mittens by Ull Tagesson

⌃ Vuokko's Klövsjö sheep and yarn

Photos ©Vuokko Hoglin

⌃ Veronika by Ebba Stålhandske

Photos courtesy of Östergötlands Ullspinneri

➢ Swatch knit from Vuokko Hoglin's handspun Klövsjö yarn

SW photo

entrepreneurs. Visitors are welcome at the factory store and gallery (hours on website). All of the Östergötlands Ullspinneri yarns are sourced from Swedish sheep, although they are undifferentiated by breed.

The Ullspinneri offers residential courses at Slöjdvillan I Stora Åby in knitting and weaving. This is the yarn company used by Ivar Asplund for some of the designs in his book *Sticka Flätor* (*Cable Knits from Nordic Lands* in English from Trafalgar Press).

Östergötlands Ullspinneri has a wide variety of yarns available, all from Swedish sources. Their yarns also are found in many shops around the country and are exported to Japan. They also offer many knitting kits through their online shop, including very innovative patterns for sweaters.

You can place an order on their website for which you will receive an invoice (currency transfers can be made through international online banking institutions).

SheepShopen

http://www.sheepshopen.n.nu/

Vuokko and her husband Jonas left Stockholm some years ago and purchased a farm in Småland (southeastern Sweden) to participate in the Swedish native sheep conservation program raising *Klövsjö*. Their products include wool-filled pillows and baby bedding, felt, sheepskins, fleece, and handspun yarn. Particularly nice are the variegated black and white yarns that produce a knitted pattern of randomly organized black, greys and white. They also have some brown sheep (somewhat unusual for the breed).

The couple has renovated their 1938 farmhouse to include a Bed and Breakfast enterprise and you can even make arrangements with Vuokko to learn to spin during a stay at the farm. While their website is not set up as an online sales shop, they are happy to ship products on request.

Knitting with SheepShopen yarns

All of the yarns provided by SheepShopen are hand spun by Vuokko, and as I mentioned in the section about *Klövskö* sheep, very fun to knit. Since I already had an idea about the fiber from working with Josefin's handspun, I was looking forward to seeing how a different spinner would approach this fleece. I met up with Vuokko at the wool festival in Kil, and her enthusiasm

and obvious love for her sheep was fully evident. I caught her excitement right away and felt the joy in her yarn making in every stitch of my swatch. Watching that random striping and pooling of the different colors form in the fabric was amazing. I had to make just one more row, and then just one more row… it was addictive. I also asked her to bring me enough fleece to spin for a sweater, and that will be one of my projects soon. With a little effort, I'm going to try to do a little Vuokko channeling and make some very happy yarn.

Solkunstens Spinnverkstad

Virövägen 10, 761 75 Norrtälje
https://www.solkustens-spinnverkstad.com/hem

Solkunstens is a well-known Spinning mill about 45 miles northeast of Stockholm. Their primary business is lönspinning, and they produce *Finull, Jamtland, Leicester* and *Gotland* wool in their mill. Most of their yarns are blended Swedish breeds and are of consistent quality. You will find their products primarily at festivals and fairs, and occasionally on their website.

Knitting with Solkunstens Yarns

I tried two different yarns from Solkunstens and found that the processing was really different from one to the other. The first was a white *Jämtland* wool singles, that certainly lives up to the reputation for incredible softness. The problem I found was that the spinning was pretty uneven, resulting in yarn with obvious thick and thin spots. Had I been expecting that (there was no information on the website suggesting that this was more

of an "art" yarn), I might have felt differently about the outcome of the swatch. As it is, I think the result is a little lumpy looking.

Solkunsten's 75/25 *Gotlands/Finull* mix (singles) is a really pretty yarn. I chose a light-grey color that has a tweedy look because of the white *Finull* that stands out clearly in the yarn. I don't usually knit swatches in garter, but I thought it might be interesting to emphasize the little points of white in the yarn. While still a little rustic in feel, I wouldn't have a problem making a sweater out of this yarn, although I'd probably go for a 2-ply to get better wear. It's a very nice yarn, and unlike the *Jämtland*, is beautifully even in the spin.

Stenkyrka Spinning Mill

Garde 176, 624 42 Tingstäde
https://www.ullspinneri.se/

Knitting with Stenkyrka Yarns

In addition to the *Texel* yarn described on page 66, I also swatched *Gotland* and the local alpaca. Stenkyrka offers both natural brown and white, although the wool from the white alpaca animals comes from the mainland rather than Gotland Island. This is a rather heavy 2-ply (11 wpi at the low end of worsted weight). It is, of course, very soft. Alpaca yarn feels heavy and dense compared to most of the Swedish yarns I've tested. You will find it very warm if you use it for a sweater. My feeling was that the Stenkyrka alpaca was pretty fuzzy. There were lots of little hairs poking out before I started knitting, and more when I finished. Blocking made the fibers bloom, so I'm

◁ Swatches from a selection of Stenkyrka yarn
SW photo

◁ With Sandy, Petr, and a small flock of Helsinge sheep

Bruce Nappi, photographer

◁ Batt from Helsinge sheep
Photo courtesy of Swedish Fibre

wondering how well this will wear. I didn't do any abrasion testing, but it's something I'd do if I was considering this for gloves or any type of garment that would get extensive wear. That being said, it is very pretty and nice to work with, and I think I'd consider using what I have left as thrums in a mitten with its nice cocoa color.

Swedish Fibre

https://www.swedishfibre.com/
https://www.etsy.com/se-en/shop/SwedishFibre

The Swedish Fibre website is the place where I began my journey into rare breed wool. Sandy Zetterlund is working hard to source as many of the heritage breeds as possible to stock in her online Etsy shop. She is dedicated to supporting the breeding program and of getting better prices for the wool itself for the farmers. She also is a stickler for quality, refusing fleece with second cuts.

Because Sandy works directly with shepherds who often have only a few sheep, the products in her shop are sometimes limited. On the other hand, she has fleece that you wouldn't easily find elsewhere. It's important to stop by her shop frequently to see what is new.

Knitting with Swedish Fibre Yarn

This *Finull* yarn was one of the first I tried of the various breeds, and I'm afraid it spoiled me completely. Soft? Oh yes. Easy to knit? Absolutely. But best of all, incredible stitch definition. I usually hesitate to work cables on this dark color of yarn but the skein literally took that decision out of my hands. I'm adding more of this to my stash with a warm winter shawl in mind. I'm thinking

⋀ Svärdsjö *(left)* and Åsen *fleece (right)*
Photos courtesy of Swedish Fibre

⋀ Swedish Fiber Finull *swatch*
SW photo

⋏ *In addition to 2- and 3-ply yarns, the Ullcentrum stock includes z-ply, Lovikka yarns, roving, and yarns on cones.*

Courtesy of Ullcentrum Öland

about knitting a cable band for the bottom edge and then picking up stitches and working up to the bind-off edge where hopefully I'll have enough left for an i-cord to give the edge some weight.

Ullcentrum

https://www.ullcentrum.com/?lang=en

Ann Linderhjelm is one of the Swedes who for years has been distressed by the amount of wool being thrown away or burned by farmers for lack of a market. With her deep interest in natural materials and understanding of the need to produce clean, environmentally friendly products, she set up Ullcentrum in 1988 determined to supervise and control all aspects of natural fiber production. She soon found, however, that the washing process took a unique set of skills best left to other professionals, and thus settled on the yarn production itself. Ann has built Ullcentrum into a large and successful business, with outlets throughout Sweden as well as in Europe, Japan and the US.

Ullcentrum collects wool regionally (from Ölalnd, Småland and Bleckinge); all Swedish wools but blended

to achieve uniform consistency. They also have some yarns made solely of *Gotland* fleece. Yarns are available in cones, as well as lace-weight through 3-ply worsted, in a multitude of solid and variegated colors suitable for knitting, crochet and weaving. In addition they also market felted wool and knitted products, and have introduced linen clothing and yarn to their line. All of the products they offer are designed in-house, and their aim is to continue to develop and improve traditional, useful and sustainable products. By interviewing local, elderly women, and researching patterns from the region, Ullcentrum knitting patterns (available free with yarn purchases) provide a new outlet for traditional Öland designs. One such design, *Blommer och Väderkvarn (Flowers & Windmill)* by Ann Linderhjelm, can be found on page 115.

Knitting with Ullcentrum Yarn

The Ullcentrum 2-ply (18-19 WPI; light sport weight) is a sturdy and strong yarn that is excellent for colorwork. It has many of the same characteristics as the Shetland yarns, with excellent stitch definition and a rustic "crunchy" feel. While it is not soft to work with, it does soften with washing and wear. My version of *Blommer och Väderkvarn* knit up very quickly on 3mm (US 2.5) needles. The mill supplies 50-gram skeins of this yarn in two-color pairs for mittens and hats.

⋏ *Blommer och Väderkvarn knit with 2-ply Ullcentrum yarn*

SW photo

ÖLAND ISLAND

Öland, the second largest island in Sweden, is located just off of the southeast coast of the mainland. The iconic windmills and numerous wildflowers create an engaging rocky landscape, also known for numerous Viking era archeological sites.

⋏ *Typical Öland windmill*

   Photo by Wigulf

The archeology of Öland is dominated by gravefields spanning the Bronze, Iron and Viking ages. The most recognized is the Gettlinge Ship burial. The custom was to surround the grave with standing stone in the shape of a boat. There are several other sites of this type including on at Anundshög, Bohuslän and Boge (on Gotland Island).

The southern part of the island is a vast limestone plane, called an alvar, which is the habitat for a huge range of rare plants including some 6,000 orchids. That area was made famous by the visit of the botanist Carl Linnaeus in 1741. Together with 6 of his students, he documented 100 previously unrecorded plants on Öland and Gotland islands. The purpose of his research was medicinal plants, but he also received support to research dye plants across Sweden.

⋏ *Rock rose*

Photo courtesy of Deborah McMillan

The island, Öland is able to support only a small number of the sheep needed to fulfill the needs of Ullcentrum. You will find cattle and the occasional alpaca grazing on the alvar farms as well as the more lush forested lands to the north.

➤ *Öland Sheep*

⋏ *Gettlinge Stone Ship Burial*

Wikipedia Commons

⋏ *Öland Forest*

Kennerth Kullman, Shutterstock image

UllForum

https://yarnsandbarns.com

UllForum has as its motto, "a small spinning mill with great ambition," and has an interesting history. The mill itself used to be part of the local agricultural college and accepted fleece from local shepherds to be spun on a lönspinning basis. After the school determined that the business was insufficiently

Photos courtesy of Ullform Spinneri, makers of UllRika yarn (Yarns & Barns)

profitable, members of the community banded together to purchase the mill and develop a locally sustainable operation. UllForum's *Yarns & Barns* features the beautiful, soft wool of the local *Jämtland* sheep. Their products are available in Stockholm at Makeri 14 and Föreningen för Svensk Hemslöjd, and several other locations around the country. It also is available in their online boutique, including the natural colored yarns, and patterns that are derived from old local designs. They also offer fleece and roving for handspinning. UllForum has done some experimenting with natural dyes, and also may offer *Svea* wool and a *Svea/Gotland* mix when available.

With ever-changing inventory, this spinning mill is a good one to watch for new developments. Their onsite shop is open from 10–4 the last Saturday of each month in Ås, Jämtland.

⋏ *Natural dyeing at the mill*

Photos by Sara Björkebaum (@bbaumish)

Knitting with Yarns & Barns Yarns

I chose the dark brown and the creamy white Yarns & Barns *Jämtland* for a winter headband and immediately fell in love with its soft, almost spongy texture. The headband is so soft and light weight that it feels quite cozy—warm but not overly so.

⋏ *Headband knit with Yarns & Barns* Jämtland *wool*

Modeled by Leah Nappi. Lauren Nappi, photographer

The only issue I found with UllForum's spinning was an occasional break in the ply in a couple of skeins. The mill is aware of the issue and has worked very hard to correct the problem, so I don't hesitate to recommend their yarns. The fastest way around this kind of break is to do a spit splice to weld the ends together again. That might be a little extra work, but the yarn is definitely worth having in your stash.

Ullspinneriet I Brink

http://ullspinerietibrink.se

Annica Jonsson offers lönspinning services for wool, alpaca and angora. She also has production from her own sheep (a *Jämtland/Leicester* cross)

⋏ *Alpaca and lambs from Annica Jannson's flock in Östergötlands*

Courtesy of Annica Jonsson

and alpaca. Located near Linköping, this is a one-person operation, with a shop onsite. Her products are available in Sweden through her online shop at her website as well as her Facebook page. You may find her at fiber festivals like Fårfest I Kil in February/March, and the wool fair at Österbybruk in August. Annica will ship her yarns overseas (cost of yarn + tax and postage, prepaid).

Contact her directly for a visit to her lovely farm if you are in Östergötlands.

Knitting with Ullspinneriet I Brink Yarns

My first swatch of Annica's yarn was her Jåmtland lamb. There absolutely is a reason that knitters are snatching up every skein of this yarn that they can find. It is a dream to knit with, and creates a gorgeous fabric that is baby soft. I've put this one on my short list to acquire a sweater's worth in the very near future. I can't say enough good things about this yarn.

The second yarn I cast on was 75% Jåmtland/25% alpaca in a tweedy grey-brown. Again, this is a super soft yarn that has a really interesting visual character in addition to its warmth. It is softly plied, but perfectly regular, giving the stitches excellent definition.

In addition to raising her own sheep, Annica also has a flock of alpaca. Alpaca are becoming more common in Sweden, with flocks both on the mainland and on Gotland Island.

⋏ Jämtland *lamb and* Jämtland/*alpaca blend 75/25% swatches (right). Both yarns are from Annica's animals and spun at her own mill*

SW photos

Växbo Lin
Växbo 3041, 821 95 Bollnäs
https://www.vaxbolin.se/

⋏ *A few examples of Växbo yarns*

SW photo

At age 16, Hanna worked as a summer guide in the Växbo factory vowing that if it ever was available, she would buy it. She had fallen in love not only with the small mill tucked into the woods, but with the beautiful products they were making. In 2006, she and her husband Jacob Bruce did buy the mill, and continue to produce beautiful home goods, clothing, fabric and linen yarn for weaving and knitting. They offer online purchasing with DHL shipping.

Wålstedts Ullspinneri
(Formerly Wålstedts Textilverkstad AB)
Hagen 15, Dala-Floda, Dalarnas
https://www.facebook.com/walstedtstextil/

Wålstedts Textilverkstad was begun by Lennart and Mary Wålstedt in 1936 basing their yarn production on Swedish wools. In time they became very well known for working with textile artists like Helena Hernmarck, Märta Måås-Fjetterström and Alice Lund to develop specialized yarns.

Wålstedts has remained a favorite among knitters and weavers, and their location in Dalarna has given them a very direct connection to the local Swedish handcraft. Their z-ply yarns for two-end knitting are exceptional.

⋏ *Lennart Wålstedt and his flock, early 20th century*

Courtesy of the Wålstedt family

After suffering a loss in the family, the mill was forced to briefly close, but reopened in 2020 as Wålstedts Ullspinneri. Still operated by family members, they are rebuilding the business slowly, and are currently focused on their general products. They look forward to working with textile artists and crafters to meet their special needs once again. Their yarns are available onsite, and through contact from their Facebook page.

Knitting with Wålstedts Yarns

I was able to acquire some z-ply yarns just as Wålstedts Textilverkstad was closing in 2019, with the specific goal of comparing it to other Swedish z-ply products. My interest in z-ply for two-end knitting came from the difficulty of finding appropriate yarns in the US (there is only one brand I'm aware of), and finding that most of the brands do not have the same robust hand as the Wålstedts product. Roger Bush, one of the current managers of the mill credits the unique combination of fibers and spinning techniques for the character of these yarns. The mill uses two systems for spinning—one for card

yarns and one for worsted spinning. The two-end wool is a blend of *Finull*, *Leicester* and *Rya*. Unique to Wålstedts is the ability of the mill to handle and spin the very long *Rya* fleece with staples of up to 30 cm in length.

Winterliagården

https://shop.winterlia.se/sv/

Winterlia Farm is located in Jämtland (northern Sweden), and according to shepherdess Erika, it is in "the middle of nowhere." She and her husband Johan bought the farm from Johan's father in 2014, and within 5 years she had won 2 gold and 2 bronze metals for her heritage sheep fleece (as well as a gold medal for spinning).

In addition to improving the farm, increasing their garden and livestock to become more self-sufficient, expanding their shop and studio (as well as a restaurant), Erika and Johan are raising 5 breeds of sheep, including heritage *Helsinge* and *Klövsjö*. All of this and a young daughter make for a crazy life Erika calls, "her dream." Her web shop is full of yarn, roving, and a lovely selection of other items made in her studio.

▲ The herds at Winterliagården

Photo courtesy of Erika Winterlia

▲ Winterliagården swatches, Allmogefår (left) and Helsinge (right)

SW photo

Knitting with Winterliagården Yarn

I tried two different yarns from Erika's selection: *Helsinge* and a type she calls Allmogefår. I did a comparison between two different handspun *Helsinge* yarns and this one from Winterliagården, and they couldn't be more different. If you look at various breed photos you'll see how very diverse the sheep can be just in color. The fibers also vary a great deal, from very coarse to fine and semi-soft. The benefit of the mill-spun for me was the tightness of

the spin that prompted me to try cables. Interestingly, the cables didn't stand out very well because of the halo of fibers in the yarn (the scratchy bits). I did think that this might be an interesting design idea, however, if you were going for a subtle texture. Still, I can't think of this as a yarn that I'd put next to my skin.

The Allmogefår (allmogefår means "old sheep") is a mix of *Helsinge* and *Klösjö*. These two breeds have wool that is pretty similar in texture and color, and the product is a very rich dark, dark brown to black. In my opinion, this is a yarn

▲ Fleece and yarn spun from Winterliagården

Photos courtesy of Erika Winterlia

that is a bit softer than the *Helsinge*, but still quite robust and rustic. This yarn has both a hard twist and a dense feel. I immediately think this would be good for a jacket or sweater designed for a walk in the woods on a cold, fall day, knit with a tight gauge to keep out the wind.

Yllet

http://ylletinredning.se/en-GB

The flagship store for Yllet homegoods, yarn, knitting designs and woolen clothing is found in Visby on Gotland Island. Their yarns are primarily a mix of *Gotland* and Faulklands *Merino* spun in Denmark at Hjelholts Uldspinneri. Their line has expanded recently to include kid mohair/Falklands *Merino* blends in natural shades and linen from Holma Helsinglands (in Sweden).

⋎ The Yllet shop in Visby carries a full line of yarns in several weights

SW photo

Their Ullgarn wools in different weights also are available in up to 30 different colors, making them ideal for many of their stranded colorwork designs.

Knitting with Yllet Yarns

I've had the chance to get to know Yllet yarns very well, having made a sweater and a hat with their *Gotland/Falkland Islands Merino* blend. It is very good quality yarn, regular and predictable. It's also really warm and a good choice if you're thinking about something for the depth of winter. I appreciate the wide range of colors and the variety of weights.

While I find this yarn a little bit hard on the hands (i.e., scratchy), it does soften up pretty well with a good soak in wool wash during blocking. Still, it's not a next-to-skin yarn but it is one I expect I'll use again.

6 Fairs and Festivals

There are a few regularly scheduled festivals/conferences through the year to build a visit around, but there also are multiple other events to tempt you throughout the year. The best places to find small weekend craft events are postings on the *Sticka!* website (*https://www.sticka.org/*), as well as websites for a number of the museums. In particular the Upplands Museum in Uppsala (*https://www.upplandsmuseet.se/*) has a long list of activities including handcrafts courses and they have in the past co-sponsored the wool market at nearby Österbybruck. Many crafts activities can also be found at the outdoor museum Skansen (*https://www.skansen.se/*). Regional crafts organizations sponsor occasional workshops and fairs, and these often can be found on the Hemslöjden website (*https://hemslojden.org/*).

Ullmarknad I Österbybruck

https://www.facebook.com/events/540804619903529/

Österbybruck is the location of the 17th century Österby ironworks. It is a complex, known as a Vallonbruk, the social and economic building complex surrounding a forge. Walloon immigrants (from Belgium) settled this area and worked the forge, giving this region an interesting heritage. With new sponsors in 2020, the wool market is expanding its focus to include not only wool, but linen, weaving and forging. This event is normally held each year in August.

SY & Hantverks Festival (Sewing and Crafts)

https://www.syfestivalen.se/

This is a very large festival held 4 times per year, usually twice in Stockholm and then in two other cities. You'll find tons of inde yarns and hand dyes as well as multiple classes in a variety of techniques. Check the website for times, locations and ticket prices.

FÅReningen Fårfest I Kil (Sheep Festival)

http://farfestikil.com/

Fårfest, held the weekend of the 9th calendar week every year in the small town of Kil has become quite a large event. Founded in 2006, the festival has 4 functions; to promote meat, wool, and leather, and the use of sheep as landscape caretakers. With about 140 vendors as well as lectures, courses and a fashion show, there is a lot to see. Advance planning is required if you hope to attend. The town of Kil has a population of about 10,000 residents, and the festival doubles that population for 3 or 4 days. Hotel rooms are very limited, but it is possible to find space with local families who open their homes each year for an extremely reasonable price.

Yarnfest Stockholm

https://www.yarnfeststockholm.com

This large retail event is planned for either the spring or fall in Stockholm. The vendors change annually, as well as the dates, so look to their website for the latest details.

Winter Market

https://www.jokkmokksmarknad.se/en/

It will take some planning of you hope to get to the Jokkmokk Market the first weekend in February each year. Situated above the Arctic Circle, it is accessible by airports and land transportation from Finland and Sweden.

The 3-day event features open houses at artist workshops; art and photography exhibits; restaurants and food tents; and a caravan of reindeer. You can have a guided tour of the museum or a sled-dog trip to the Northern Lights complete with a 5-course meal in a Sami tent. There are also a wealth of programs for children, and endless shopping.

Accommodations in Jokkmokk are limited, but other surroundings villages offer cottages and home stays, and there is sufficient bus transportation to get back and forth fairly easily.

Ullfestival (Sparreholm)

https://www.bavensspinnhus.se/

This festival is sponsored by Båvens Spinnhus; a small event filled with activities, including a visit to the mill. Check their website to see when the next festival is planned.

7 Design Inspiration & Patterns

Needle size conversion

US	Metric (mm)	UK
000	1.5	
00	1.75	
0	2.0	14
1	2.25	13
2	2.75	12
2.5	3.0	11
3	3.25	10
4	3.5	
5	3.75	9
6	4.0	8

US	Metric (mm)	UK
7	4.5	7
8	5.0	6
9	5.5	5
10	6.0	4
10.5	6.5	3
	7	2
	7.5W	1
11	8.0	0
13	9.0	00
15	10.0	000

Yarn weights

US Craft Council Designation	Yarn Weight	Wraps/Inch
0	Lace	›35
1	Fingering	19-22
2	Sport	15-18
3	DK	14-14
4	Worsted	9-11
5	Bulky	7-8
6	Super bulky	‹6

BLOMMER OCH VÄDERKVARN (FLOWERS & WINDMILL)

By Ann Linderhjelm Pattern, courtesy of Ullcentrum

Photo courtesy of Ullcentrum

Blommer och Väderkvarn is perhaps the most well-known of all the patterns from Öland, Sweden. The pattern depicts stylized windmills and flowers Ölandssolvända (rockrose of Helianthemum oelandicum), the province flower of Öland.

Materials

- Ullcentrum's 2-ply wool yarn in 2 contrasting colors (40 g/color)
- Circular needle size US 2.5 (3mm), 16" (40 cm) in length
- Double-point needles US 2.5 (3mm) for decrease rounds
- Stitch marker
- Tapestry needle to weave in ends.

Instructions

Using the darker color cast on 132 stitches and join in the round. Mark the beginning of the round with a stitch marker.

Knit rounds for ¾" (2cm) to make a rolled edge.

Add light color and work corrugated ribbing as follows:

K1 (light), p1 (dark) for 10 rounds.

Work 1 round in the light color, and then begin working the chart below as follows:

Work rows 1–16

Work rows 17–32

Work rows 1–16

Break the dark color leaving a tail of at least 6" (15 cm) to weave in. Working in the light color, knit two rows.

Decreases

Note: switch to DPNs when necessary

Round 1: *K9, k2tog*

Round 2: Knit all stitches

Round 3: *K8, k2tog*

Round 4: Knit all stitches

Continue decrease rounds as above, knitting 1 less stitch between decreases each time until 48 stitches remain.

Break yarn, leaving a tail of at least 6" (15 cm). Thread a tapestry needle and pull the yarn through the remaining stitches. Tighten until the hole disappears, working the yarn through the stitches again and weaving the end into the inside.

Weave in all remaining ends.

Wash the hat in warm water with a wool wash. Depending on the desired size, it is possible to stretch the wool somewhat while wet. Take care not to overstretch. Lay flat or over a head-form to dry.

Photo by Lauren Nappi

BLOMMER OCH VÄDERKVARN (FLOWERS & WINDMILL)

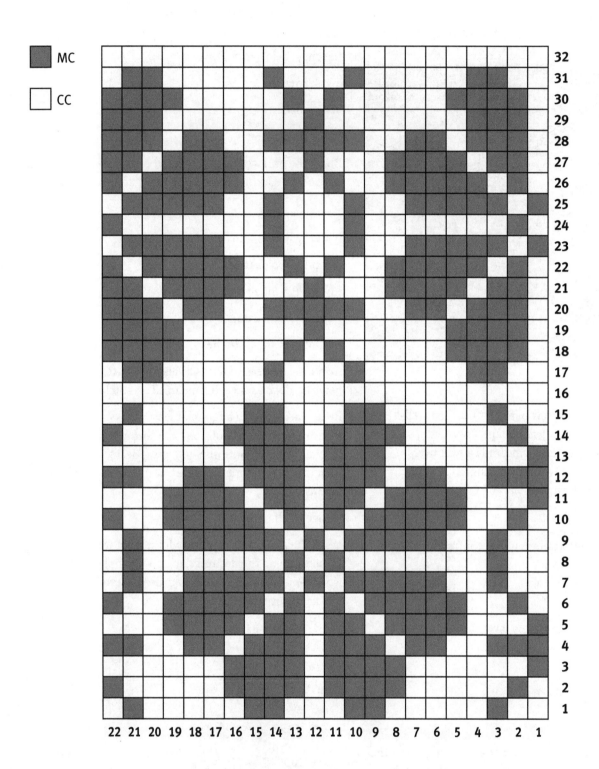

LOVIKKA-STYLE MITTENS

by Sara J Wolf

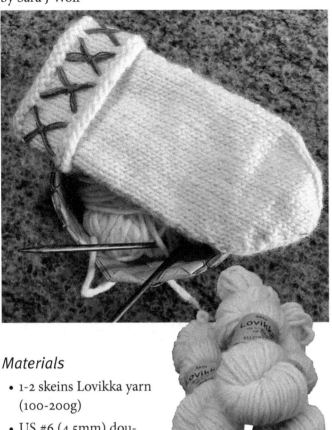

Materials

- 1-2 skeins Lovikka yarn (100-200g)
- US #6 (4.5mm) dou-ble-pointed needles
- Cotton waste yarn
- Tapestry needle
- Stitch marker (optional) to mark start of round
- 2 or more colors of wool embroidery yarn (optional)

Pattern notes: You will find many patterns for Lovikka mittens, but REAL Lovikka mittens are only knit by approved knitters in Norrbotten Province. I've seen these mittens with both pointed and rounded tops; with and without decorative stitching, and settled on this pattern as a good "average" of all of them. These mittens are very warm (and a little stiff), and you'll appreciate them on a cold winter morning.

For the best result, knit at a very tight gauge. Swatch first and calculate the number of stitches to fit your hand snuggly. Fit is important for this mitten, and your size is whatever fits. Two sizes are given as guidance, one for a S/M size, and one for a M/L size. It is easiest to start with a number of stitches divisible by 4 to make the decreases easy.

The mitten is knit on needles quite a bit smaller than is normal for the thickness of the yarn to make the fabric firm and wind-proof. The mitten itself should be quite snug, but not so tight that it's hard to bend the hand. You are encouraged to swatch in the round to establish the fit. If the S/M is just a little snug, try the next size larger needle rather than adding stitches. Or, since there is a difference of 2 stitches/needle between sizes, consider adding only 1 stitch/needle. The instructions for the S/M are given first, with the instructions for M/L in parenthesis as follows: "Cast on 28 (36) stitches and divide evenly on 4 needles."

Instructions for Left Mitten

Using the long-tail method, cast on 28 (36) stitches and arrange on 4 needles [7 (9) stitches on each needle].

Join to work in the round, taking care not to twist, and placing a stitch marker at the beginning of the round if desired.

Round 1: Knit all stitches

Round 2: Purl all stitches

Knit 8 (10) more rounds. Turn inside out to form the cuff, and continue knitting in the round until the work is 4.5" (5") to the turn.

On the final row, knit the last 5 (7) stitches onto waste yarn of a different color to mark the thumb. Place those 5 (7) stitches back onto the left needle and knit again with the working yarn.

Continue knitting in the round until the work is 2.5" (2.75") beyond the waste yarn.

NOTE: *Measure your hand from the base of the thumb to the top of your middle finger. The decrease rows are between 1.5" and 2" in depth, so make sure to begin those rows 1.5" to 2" from the top of the middle finger based on your hand measurement.*

Decrease Rounds

Round 1

Needle 1: K1, k2tog, knit to the end of the needle.

Needle 2: Knit to the last 3 stitches. K2tog, K1.

Needle 3: as needle 1

Needle 4: as needle 2

Round 2

Knit all stitches

Continue working rounds 1 and 2 until there are 4 stitches remaining on each needle

Work round 1 twice (2 stitches remaining on each needle).

Break yarn, leaving a tail of at least 6". Thread a tapestry needle with the tail and pull it through all of the stitches. Pull tightly, take the tail to the inside, and fasten off by weaving the end through the backs of the stitches.

Thumb

Remove the waste yarn and place the 10 (14) stitches plus 2 stitches to close the gap onto 4 needles. Join the yarn and begin to knit in the round. Continue until the thumb is 1.75" to 2" in length.

Decrease as follows: K2 together at the beginning of needle 1, end of needle 2, beginning of needle 3 and end of needle 4 (4 stitches decreased).

Knit 1 round.

Work decrease round again so that 4 (8) stitches remain.

- For size S/M: Break yarn leaving a 6" tail. Thread a tapestry needle with the tail and pull it through all of the stitches. Pull tightly, take the tail to the inside, and fasten off by weaving the end through the backs of the stitches.
- For size M/L: Work one additional decrease row (4 stitches remain). Finish off as for size S/M.

Instructions for Right Mitten

Work instructions 1-5 as for Left mitten.

On the final row, knit needle one. On needle 2 knit the last 5 (7) stitches on waste yarn. Place those stitches back on the left needle and knit again with the working yarn.

Continue from instruction #7 as for the Left Mitten.

Finishing

Weave in the ends from the cast-on edge.

Soak in warm water with a wool wash. Squeeze out excess and block to dry.

Brush interior and exterior surfaces gently to raise the knap.

Decorate the cuff with wool embroidery designs if desired.

BLOOD MOON SHAWL

by Kristin Blom

Gauge

- 17 sts / 34 rows = 10 cm x 10 cm / 4"x 4" over stocking stitch on 4 mm/US 6 needles after blocking.

Materials

- Mohair Toni (72% Kid Mohair, 28% Silk), Dandelion Yarns, 400 m /437 y per 100 g/3.5 oz. Yarn A: Red: 1.5 skeins. Yarn B: Dusty pink: 1 skein
- 4 mm/US6 circular needles, 100 cm/40" in length. Always use a needle size that will result in the correct tension after blocking.
- tapestry needle
- 10 stitch markers

The shawl sample photographed for this pattern is knitted using mohair/silk yarn from Dandelion Yarns. These colors are available as a limited number of kits from Makeri14, where you can also find assorted colors from Stockholm Woolery.

Note on yarn: Stockholm Woolery - Mohair on Silk is dyed on the same base as the Mohair Toni, so makes for an easy substitute yarn. The original yarn is 400m per 100g. If substituting, try and stay close to that, with a preferences to going a bit thicker yarn rather than thinner. The structural design of the shawl might be lost if the yarn is too thin.

Note on metrage/yardage: If you are working precisely to gauge, you can just pull this shawl off with two balls of yarn (one of each color). However, if you wind up working any looser, you will end up needing to play yarn chicken with Yarn A, not be able to work the full number of stripes described and/or use more of Yarn B. This will depend on how tight or loose you knit. If you want to be safe, go for three balls, but if you have two at home and can't wait to cast on and you're willing to improvise, go for it! You can always add a little of a third color for the bind-off—a contrasting color could frame the shawl nicely.

Note on colors: You can go for three skeins in three different colors as well if you prefer, and play around with color combinations. For example, you can make the stripes in two colors and the blocks in between in the third, or one block in each color and stripe randomly between.

Special Techniques

German Short Rows

The short rows in this pattern are based on using the German Short Row technique which is the simplest to use in this context, but frustratingly difficult to learn from a text. If you don't already know how to do German Short Rows, I recommend you learn from YouTube: I was surprised of how easy it was! The basic idea is that you do the opposite of the Wrap and Turn method short rows, by first 'Turning' AND THEN 'Wrapping'. First you 'Turn' your work, bringing your yarn IN FRONT OF YOUR NEEDLE and then bring it backwards over the needle (to 'Wrap'), so that the first st looks distorted (as if it has two legs)—this is a Double Stitch (DS). You slip this Double Stitch, and work the next stitch firmly. Whenever passing a DS, you work it like any normal st, being careful to work both strands/legs together. Do not treat them as two sts to work separately.

I-Cord Bind-Off

Using the cable cast-on method, cast on 3 sts in the first st on your left needle (knit one st in the first st, move it over to the left needle, knit another st in the new st, move it over to the left needle, repeat for one more st) - now you have 3 new sts on your left needle. These 4 sts will become your i-cord. As you work each row/round, you will knit the final st of your i-cord together with a live st from the edge of the shawl to attach them together.

Each row/round: [K3, ssk, slip 4 sts purlwise from right to left needle], repeat to end of row. When you have just the 4 i-cord sts left, with no more live sts remaining along the shawl edge, cut the yarn and pull it through all 4 sts and pull tight. Secure end.

Garter-Tab Cast-On

With Yarn A, using your prefered method, cast on 3 sts. Work 9 rows in garter stitch. Leaving 3 sts live, pick up and knit 5 sts along the long side of the tab, and a further 3 sts from the cast-on edge. 11 sts

Section 1: Set-Up Rows

Whole section worked with Yarn A.

Row 1 (WS): Purl to end.

Row 2 (RS) (inc): Kfb to end. 11 sts inc, 22 sts

Row 3: K3, p16, k3.

Row 4 (RS) (inc): K3, PM, kfb, PM, [k2, PM] x 7, kfb, PM, k3. 2 sts inc, 24 sts

Note on markers: If nothing else is specified, simply slip markers as you pass them.

Row 5: K3, purl to last marker, k3.

Note: Rows 3- 5 establish the 3-st garter stitch edges that will be worked consistently to until the Half Moon Edging.

Stocking Stitch

Row 1 (RS) (inc): K3, SM, [kfb x 2, SM] repeat to last M, k3. 18 sts inc, 42 sts

Row 2: K3, purl to last marker, k3.

Row 3: Knit to end.

Row 4: K3, purl to last marker, k3.

Rows 5-8: Repeat Rows 3-4 twice more.

Row 9 (RS) (inc): K3, SM, [k1, M1L, k3, M1R, SM] x 9, k3. 18 sts inc, 60 sts

Row 10: K3, purl to last marker, k3.

Rows 11-14: Repeat Rows 3-4 twice more.

Row 15 (RS) (inc): K3, SM, [k1, M1L, knit to next M, M1R, SM] x 9, k3. 18 sts inc, 78 sts

Row 16: K3, purl to last marker, k3.

Rows 17-20: Repeat Rows 3-4 twice more.

Row 21 (RS) (inc): K3, SM, [k1, M1L, knit to next M, M1R, SM] x 9, k3. 18 sts inc, 96 sts

Row 22: K3, purl to last marker, k3.

Rows 23-34: Repeat Rows 3-4 another 6 times.

Section 2: Stripes

Attach Yarn B, don't cut Yarn A.

Row 1 (RS) (inc): K3, SM, [sl1wyib, knit to next M, SM] x 8, sl1wyib, k7, kfb, remove and replace final M here, sl1wyib, k3. 1 st inc, 97 sts

Row 2 (WS): K3, sl1wyif, SM, [knit to 1 st before next M, sl1wyif, SM] x 9, k3.

With Yarn A:
Row 3: Knit all sts.

Row 4: K3, p1, [knit to 1 st before next M, p1, SM] x 9, k3.

With Yarn B:
Row 5: K3, SM, [sl1wyib, knit to next M, SM] to last M, SM, sl1wyib, k3.

Row 6: K3, sl1wyif, SM, [knit to 1 st before next M, sl1wyif, SM] x 9, k3.

With Yarn A:
Row 7 (RS) (inc): K3, SM, [k1, kfb, knit to 1 st before next M, kfb, SM] x 9, k4. 18 sts inc, 115 sts

Row 8: K3, p1, [knit to 1 st before next M, p1] to last M, SM, k3.

Rows 9-20: *Repeat Rows 5-6 with Yarn B. Repeat Rows 3-4 with Yarn A.* Repeat from * to * twice more.

With Yarn B:
Rows 21-22: Repeat Rows 5-6.

With Yarn A:
Rows 23-24: Repeat Rows 7-8. 18 sts inc, 133 sts

Rows 25-36: *Repeat Rows 5-6 with Yarn B. Repeat Rows 3-4 with Yarn A.* Repeat from * to * twice more.

You have worked 18 garter ridge stripes in total in this section. Break Yarn A.

Section 3: Stocking Stitch

Whole section worked with Yarn B.

Row 1 (RS) (inc): K3, SM, [k1, p1, M1L, knit to 1 before next M, M1R, p1, SM] x 9, k4. 18 sts inc, 151 sts

Row 2 (WS): K3, p1, SM [k1, purl to 2 sts before next M, k1, p1, SM] to last M, k3.

Row 3: K3, SM, [sl1wyib, p1, knit to 1 st before next M, p1, SM] repeat to last M, sl1wyib, k3.

Row 4: K3, sl1wyif, SM, [k1, purl to 2 sts before next M, k1, sl1wyif, SM] x 9, SM, k3.

Row 5: K3, SM, [k1, p1, knit to 1 st before next M, p1, SM] x 9, k4.

Row 6: K3, p1, SM [k1, purl to 2 sts before next M, k1, p1, SM] to last M, k3.

Row 7 (RS) (inc): K3, SM, [sl1wyib, p1, M1L, knit to 1 st before next M, M1R, p1, SM] repeat to last M, sl1wyib, k3.

18 sts inc, 169 sts

Row 8 (WS): K3, sl1wyif, SM, [k1, purl to 2 sts before next M, k1, sl1wyif, SM] to last M, k3.

Rows 9-16: *Repeat Rows 5-6. Repeat Rows 3-4.*

Repeat from * to * once more.

Rows 17-18: Repeat Rows 1-2. 18 sts inc, 187 sts

Rows 19-20: Repeat Rows 3-4.

Rows 21-28: *Repeat Rows 5 and 6. Repeat Rows 3 and 4.*

Repeat from * to * once more.

Rows 29-30: Repeat Rows 1-2. 18 sts inc, 205 sts

Section 4: Stripes

Don't cut Yarn B. Reattach Yarn A.

With Yarn A:
Row 1 (RS): K3, SM, [sl1wyib, knit to next M, SM] to last M, sl1wyib, k3.

Row 2 (WS): K3, sl1wyif, SM, [knit to 1 st before next M, sl1wyif, SM], repeat to last M, k3.

With Yarn B:
Row 3: Knit to end.

Row 4: K3, p1, [knit to 1 st before next M, p1, SM] to last M, k3.

With Yarn A:
Rows 5-6: Repeat Rows 1-2.

With Yarn B:
Rows 7-8: Repeat Rows 3-4.

With Yarn A:
Rows 9-10: Repeat Rows 1-2.

With Yarn B:
Row 11 (inc): K3, SM, [k1, kfb, knit to 1 st before next M, kfb, SM], repeat to last M, k4. 18 sts inc, 223 sts

Row 12: K3, p1, SM, [knit to 1 st before next M, p1, SM] to last M, k3.

With Yarn A:
Rows 13-14: Repeat Rows 1-2.

With Yarn B:
Rows 15-16: Repeat Rows 3-4.

With Yarn A:
Rows 17-18: Repeat Rows 1-2.

With Yarn B:
Rows 19-20: Repeat Rows 11-12. 18 sts inc, 241 sts

Rows 21-28: *Repeat Rows 1-2 with Yarn A. Repeat Rows 3-4 with Yarn B.* Repeat from * to * once more.

With Yarn A:
Rows 29-30: Repeat Rows 1-2.

With Yarn B:
Rows 31-32: Repeat Rows 11-12. 18 sts inc, 259 sts

With Yarn A:
Rows 33-34: Repeat Rows 1-2.

With Yarn B:
Rows 35-36: Repeat Rows 3 and 4.

You have worked 18 garter ridge stripes in total in this section. Break Yarn B.

Section 5: Stocking Stitch

Whole section worked with Yarn A.

Row 1: K3, [SM, k1, p1, knit to 1 st before next M, p1] repeat to last M, SM, k4.

Row 2: K3, p1, [k1, purl to 2 sts before next M, k1, p1, SM] to last M, k3.

Row 3: K3, SM, [sl1wyib, p1, knit to 1 st before next M, p1, SM] repeat to last M, sl1wyib, k3.

Row 4: K3, sl1wyif, SM, [k1, purl to 2 sts before next M, k1, sl1wyif, SM] repeat to last M, k3.

Row 5 (RS) (inc): K3, SM, [k1, p1, M1L, knit to 1 st

before next M, M1R, p1, SM] repeat to last M, k4.

18 sts inc, 277 sts

Row 6 (WS): K3, p1, SM, [k1, purl to 2 sts before next M, k1, p1, SM] to last M, k3.

Rows 7-8: Repeat Rows 3-4.

Rows 9-16: *Repeat Rows 1-2. Repeat Rows 3-4.*

Repeat from * to * once more.

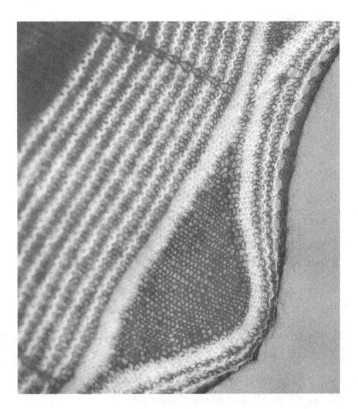

Rows 17-18: Repeat Rows 5-6. 18 sts inc, 295 sts

Rows 19-20: Repeat Rows 3-4.

Rows 21-28: *Repeat Rows 1-2. Repeat Rows 3-4.*

Repeat from * to * one more time.

Rows 29-30: Repeat Rows 1-2.

Rows 31-32: Repeat Rows 5-6. 18 sts inc, 313 sts

Section 6: Stripes

Reattach Yarn B. Don't break Yarn A.

With Yarn B:
Row 1 (RS): K3, SM, [sl1wyib, knit to next M, SM] to last M, SM, sl1wyib, k3.

Row 2 (WS): K3, sl1wyif, SM, [knit to 1 st before next M, sl1wyif, SM] x 9, k3.

With Yarn A:
Row 3: Knit to end.

Row 4: K3, p1, SM, [knit to 1 st before next M, p1, SM] to last M, k3.

With Yarn B:
Rows 5-6: Repeat Rows 1-2.

With Yarn A:
Row 7-8: Repeat Rows 3-4.

With Yarn B:
Row 9-10: Repeat Rows 1-2.

With Yarn A:
Row 11 (RS) (inc): K3, SM, [k1, kfb, knit to 1 st before next M, kfb, SM], repeat to last M, k4. 18 sts inc, 331 sts

Row 12: K3, p1, SM, [knit to 1 st before next M, p1, SM] to last M, k3.

Rows 13-24:

Repeat Rows 1-2 with Yarn B. Repeat Rows 3-4 with Yarn A. Repeat from * to * twice more.

With Yarn B:
Rows 25-26: Repeat Rows 1-2.

With Yarn A:
Rows 27-28: Repeat Rows 11-12. 18 sts inc, 349 sts

With Yarn B:
Rows 29-30: Repeat Rows 1-2.

With Yarn A:

Rows 31-32: Repeat Rows 3-4.

With Yarn B:

Rows 33-34: Repeat Rows 1-2.

With Yarn A:

Rows 35-36: Repeat Rows 1-2. 18 sts inc, 367 sts

Do not break yarns.

You have worked 18 garter ridge stripes in total in this section.

You have 40 sts between Markers except before first Marker (3 sts) and after last Marker (4 sts).

Section 7: Half Moon Edging

With Yarn B, work 4 rows of stocking stitch. Twist Yarns A and B together at the edge on each RS to carry Yarn A

to where you will next use it - you will be using both yarns again shortly.

From here on you are not working the 3-st garter stitch edges anymore.

Note on Short Rows: This pattern is calculated for German Short Rows and if you use another method take care to make the turnings in the same place as mentioned below.

With Yarn A:

Next Row (RS): K3, SM, [k35 (until you have 5 unworked sts before the M), turn work (that is knitting from the WS), DS, p29, turn, DS, k28, turn, DS, p27, turn, DS, continue working short rows as set until you reach the last worked st, turn, DS, and continue until you have 5 unworked sts in the middle (on the WS), work these 5 sts, turn, DS, knit all sts from the RS (take care to knit both strands of DS together), until you reach next M, SM] repeat to last M, SM, knit to end.

Next Row (WS): Purl to end, taking care to purl both strands of the wrapped sts together as you pass them.

With Yarn B:

Work 2 rows of stocking stitch.

Next Row (RS) (inc): K3, SM, k1, [(k8, M1R) x 2, k6, M1L, k8, M1L, k7, sl2, remove M, k1, PSSO (both slipped

sts), PM] x 8, (k8, M1R) x 2, k6, M1L, k8, M1L, knit to end. 20 sts inc, 387 sts

Next Row:

Purl to end.

With Yarn A:

Work 2 rows of garter stitch.

With Yarn B:

Next Row (dec): K3, remove M, [knit to 1 st before next M, sl1, remove M, sl1, k1, PSSO (both slipped sts)] x 8, knit to last M, remove M, knit to end. 16 sts dec, 371 sts

Next Row: Knit to end.

With Yarn A:

Next 2 Rows: Work for garter stitch.

With Yarn B:

Next 2 Rows: Work for garter stitch. Cut Yarn B.

With Yarn A:

Next Row: [K2tog, YO] to last st, k1.

Next Row: Knit to end.

Bind-Off

With Yarn A, cable cast on 3 sts in the first st on your left needle and work an i-cord bind-off (see Special Techniques Section). Break yarn.

Finishing

Weave in all ends.

Special Blocking Instructions

Soak in lukewarm water with a yarn-friendly detergent. Squeeze gently (don't wring!) Put the shawl inside a big, dry towel and squeeze out extra water. Block the shawl by first stretching out the upper part and securing it with pins, then stretch the shawl out evenly to form a half circle, add blocking wires and/or pins just above the halfmoon edge. Finish off by pulling out each half-moon at the bottom and securing it with pins.

LADIES SWEATER WITH FLOWERS

by Katarina Segerbrand

Ull Alderin, photographer

Gauge

- 28 sts and 32 rows = 10 x 10 cm pattern using 3,5 mm needles.

Materials

- Alpacka solo (100 % alpaca. 50 g = approx 167 m) from JÄRBO GARN, *www.jarbo.se*
- Circular needles, 3 mm, length 40 cm. 3 and 3,5 mm, length 60 cm
- Double point needles, 3 and 3,5 mm (if you prefer to work the sleeves in rounds)

Yarn Usage

- Col 1: 300 (300) 350 (400) 450 (500) g (col 29135, light grey)
- Col 2: 50 (50) 50 (50) 50 (50) g (col 29125, green)
- Col 3: 50 (50) 50 (50) 50 (50) g (col 29117, rust)
- Col 4: 50 (50) 50 (50) 50 (50) g (col 29123, orange)
- Col 5: 50 (50) 50 (50) 50 (50) g (col 29126, pink)
- Col 6: 50 (50) 50 (50) 50 (50) g (col 29127, yellow green)

Sizes

Ladies/mens: XS (S, M, L, XL, 2XL)

- Sizes (EU): 32–34 (36–38, 40–42, 44–46, 48–50, 52–54)
- Length: 55 (57, 59, 61, 63, 65) cm
- Width: 85 (92, 99, 109, 124, 135) cm
- Sleeve length: 45 (46, 47, 48, 49, 50) cm

Back and Front

Using 3 mm circular needle and col 1, cast on 238 (258, 278, 306, 346, 378) sts.

Work 7 rounds rib k1, p1. Place a marker on each side to denote back and front.

Sts 119 (129, 139, 153, 173, 189) respectively.

Now work K every round until work measures 4 (6, 7, 9, 10, 12) cm.

Dec 1 st at each side the markers = 4 sts decreased.

Repeat the decreases every 3rd cm 4 times.

Work 3 rnds.

Now increase 1 st each side of marker = 4 sts increased.

Repeat the increases every 6th cm 4 times.

Continue even until work measures 33, 34, 35, 36, 37, 38) cm.

Change to 3.5 mm circular needle and work in pattern following the chart, back and front begin and end in the same way.

When the chart is completed change to 3 mm circular needle and work in col 1 until end of work. At the same time, divide in back and front when work measures 39 (40, 41, 42, 43, 44) cm and work rows backwards and forwards.

Back: Bind off

XS: 5-3-2-2-2-1-1-1

S: 5-3-2-2-2-1-1-1-1-1-1

M: 6-3-2-2-2-1-1-1-1-1-1

L: 6-3-2-2-2-1-1-1-1-1-1-1-1-1-1

XL: 7-3-2-2-2-2-1-1-1-1-1-1-1-1-1-1-1

2XL: 7-3-2-2-2-2-2-1-1-1-1-1-1-1-1-1-1-1-1-1-1) sts each side for armholes.

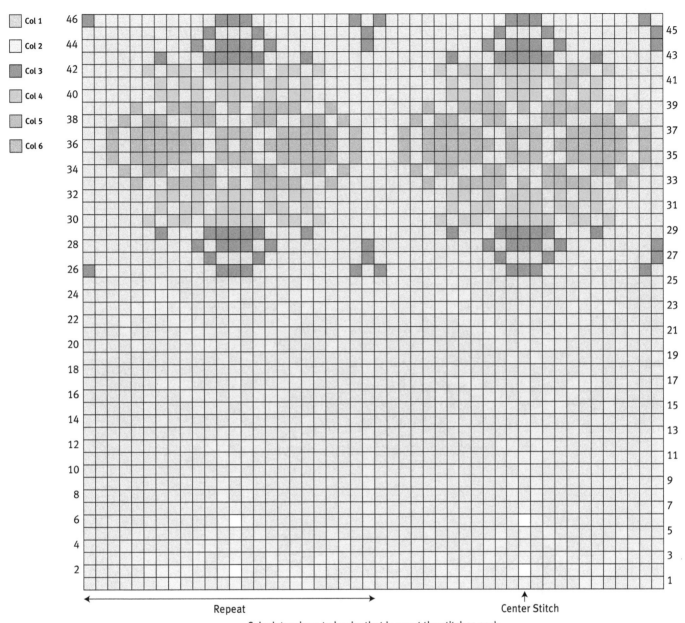

Col 1
Col 2
Col 3
Col 4
Col 5
Col 6

Repeat

Center Stitch

Calculate where to begin, that is count the stitches each
side of the center stitch to denote where to begin and end.
Back and front begin and end the same way

Work even until back measures 53 (55, 57, 59, 61, 63) cm.

Slip center 39 (39, 43, 43, 45, 45) sts onto a holder (neck sts), work each side separately.

Bind off 2-1-1 sts at neck edge. Slip shoulder sts onto a holder for 3-needle bind off. Back should measure 55 (57, 59, 61, 63, 65) cm.

Front: Bind off for armholes in the same way as back. Work even until front measures 46 (48, 50, 52, 54, 56) cm.

Slip center 29 (29, 33, 33, 35, 35) m onto a holder (neck sts), work each side separately. Bind off 2-2-2-1-1-1 sts at neck edge. Front should measure 55 (57, 59, 61, 63, 65) cm. Slip shoulder sts onto a holder for 3-needle bind off.

Please read through the complete sleeve pattern before start just so you don't miss any detail.

Cast on 2 sts less (selvage sts) if you work the sleeves on double point needles.

Sleeves

With 3 mm needles and col 1 cast on 58 (58, 62, 62, 64, 64) sts.

Work 7 rows in rib k1, p1.

Change to 3.5 mm needles and continue in st st and at the same time increase 5 (5, 5, 7, 7, 7) sts evenly on 1st row. Work 3 cm even.

Sleeve increases: M1 inside the selvage st at each side, repeat increases every 3.5 (3, 3, 2.5, 2.5, 2) cm until there are 85 (89, 95, 101, 105, 111) sts on the needle.

Continue even until sleeve measures 39 (40, 41, 42, 43, 44) cm, change to 3.5 mm needles and work in pattern following the chart, taking the increased sts into pattern. After chart is completed, change to 3 mm needles and work in col 1 until sleeve is finished. Continue until sleeve measures 45 (46, 47, 48, 49, 50) cm.

Shape top

NB! Bind off at the same pattern row as back and front. Bind off 5-3-2-2-2 (5-3-2-2-2, 6-3-2-2-2, 6-3-2-2-2, 7-3-2-2-2, 7-3-2-2-2) sts each side. Decrease 1 st each side inside the selvage st on alt rows 12 (14, 16, 17, 18, 21) times.

Work 1 row.

Bind off 2 sts beg of following 4 rows.

Bind off rem 25 (25, 25, 29, 29, 29) sts.

Making Up

Block the pieces after measurments, cover with a damp cloth and let dry. Join the shoulder using invisble 3-needle bind off.

Neck edge: Using the shorter 3 mm circular needle and col 1, pick up 142 (142, 146, 146, 150, 150) sts including the stitches on holders, work 5 row in rib k1, p1.

Bind off in rib.

Sew sleeves together, using selvage st as seam allowance.

Sew sleeves into armholes.

TVÅÄNDSSTICKNING MITTEN

By Karin Kahnlund

White Mittens in Two-end Knitting

Gauge

38 stitches/10 cm (9,5 st /1 inch)

Materials

- z-plied yarn, from Wålstedts Ullspinneri, 235 m/100g. 125 gram of yarn will suffice for a pair of mittens
- Set of 5 DPNs. Recommended needle size: metric size 2.5 mm (US size 1.5) - or size required to get gauge

Size

Woman's Average

The instructions presume that you have a basic knowledge of two-end knitting.

The Right-hand Mitten

Cast-on 72 stitches, using the cast-on described below, using three white yarn-threads.

Distribute the 72 stitches on to four needles, (18 stitches on each needle).

Knit the pattern in the round according to the chart, reading the chart from right to left for every round. At the right side, the chart begins at the little-finger. The pattern on the back of the mitten-hand is knit on needles one and two.

Thumb-gusset, increased at one side

Begin the increases on row 20 - the increases are marked with an x on the chart. Always increase in the 2nd stitch on the third needle, and increase on every row, 14 times.

Knit another 10 rows without any increases. On row 45, knit through needles 1 and 2. On the third needle, knit the first stitch, then put the following 23 stitches (= gusset stitches) on a separate thread. Cast on nine (9) new stitches and knit the remaining eight (8) stitches on the third needle. Now, you should have 18 stitches on each needle once again.

Carry on knitting according to the chart until the mitten has the desired length, (approximately to the top of your little finger).

Decreasing for the top of the mitten

The braided decrease (see below) is done at the beginning of the first and the third needle. Three stitches become one stitch with each decrease. Keep decreasing on every row until you have 4 stitches left on each needle. "Snap-off" as described below.

Thumb

Put the 23 gusset stitches from the thread on two needles and pick up 9 stitches from the previously cast on stitches = 32 stitches. Regroup the stitches so that the row will begin at the point between index finger and thumb. Knit the thumb to desired length, usually to the middle of the thumbnail. Make the braided decrease until 8 stitches remain. "Snap-off" the remaining stitches.

Left-hand Mitten

Cast-on and knit in the same way as the right-hand mitten. but mirror-reverse the chart. The easiest way to do that is to read it from the left to the right.

The increases for the thumb-gusset are made in the penultimate (= last but one) stitch on the second needle.

The pattern on the back of the mitten-hand is knit on needles three and four.

Before decreasing for the mitten you can alter the stitches so that the pattern will be centered. Move the last stitch on each needle to the next needle, where it will become the first stitch. The braided decreases are done, as before, at the beginning of the 1st and 3rd needle.

Finishing

Secure all threads.

Turn the mittens inside-out. Carefully full the mittens in tepid water. Roll the mittens into a terry-cloth towel and press out the water.

Let the mittens dry on a flat surface.

Cast-On nr 1, for two-end knitting

This cast-on uses a knitting needle and three threads. Two alternating threads will make the stitches. Both these two threads are connected to the ball of yarn (one from the inside and one from the outside). The third thread is about 3,7 meters (4 yards). Make a slip-knot on the needle with all three yarns (leaving 4 - 8 inch tails) and place the short yarn-thread over your left-hand thumb.

a) Begin by holding the knitting needle in your left hand. Hold the two other yarn-threads in your right-hand, with your index-finger between them.

b) Insert the needle into the loop of yarn wrapped around your left-hand thumb.

c) Now wrap one of your right-hand yarns around the needle (in front of the thumb-yarn loop) and with your thumb bring the loop over the right hand yarn, drop the loop off your thumb and draw both threads tight. You have cast on one stitch with the first thread.

d) Make a new thumb-loop with the left-hand thread, and repeat a-c, this time using the other of the two right-hand threads. The new stitch is made with the second thread. By repeating a-d you can cast on as many stitches as you need. After all stitches you need have been cast-on, remove the slip-knot, which does not count as a stitch.

The Braided Decrease

1. Put the working needle through the far-side of the two first stitches on the next needle. With your left hand, take hold of the previous needle.

2. With your working needle, fetch the last stitch on the previous needle, and put the working needle into the last stitch, as if to purl it.

3. Pull the fetched stitch through the first two stitches. Let them off the left needle.

4. Let the fetched stitch slip off the previous needle and leave it on the working-needle.

To "Snap-Off" Stitches

When all decreases are done at the top of the mitten, you "snap-off" the last stitches. This is done in the following manner:

Decrease until you have about four stitches left on each needle. Regroup the stitches to two parallel needles; the stitches from needle 1 and 2 on one needle, and the stitches from needle 3 and 4 on the other needle. Break off the yarns so that they are about 25 cm (10 inches) long.

Thread a (blunt) needle with the yarn from the penultimate stitch. Sew through last stitch from the inside and outwards. Lift the sewn stitch off the needle.

Gather all the remaining stitches on the sewing-needle: taking every other stitch from the near-side knitting-needle, and every other stitch from the far-side knitting-needle.

Pull the thread through all the stitches. Turn. Skipping the first stitch, sew back through all the stitches again. Push the sewing-needle to the reverse side of the knitting, remove the thread and secure it.

Thread the sewing-needle with the other yarn. Skip the first stitch and sew through all the stitches once. Push the sewing-needle to the reverse side of the knitting, remove the thread and secure it.

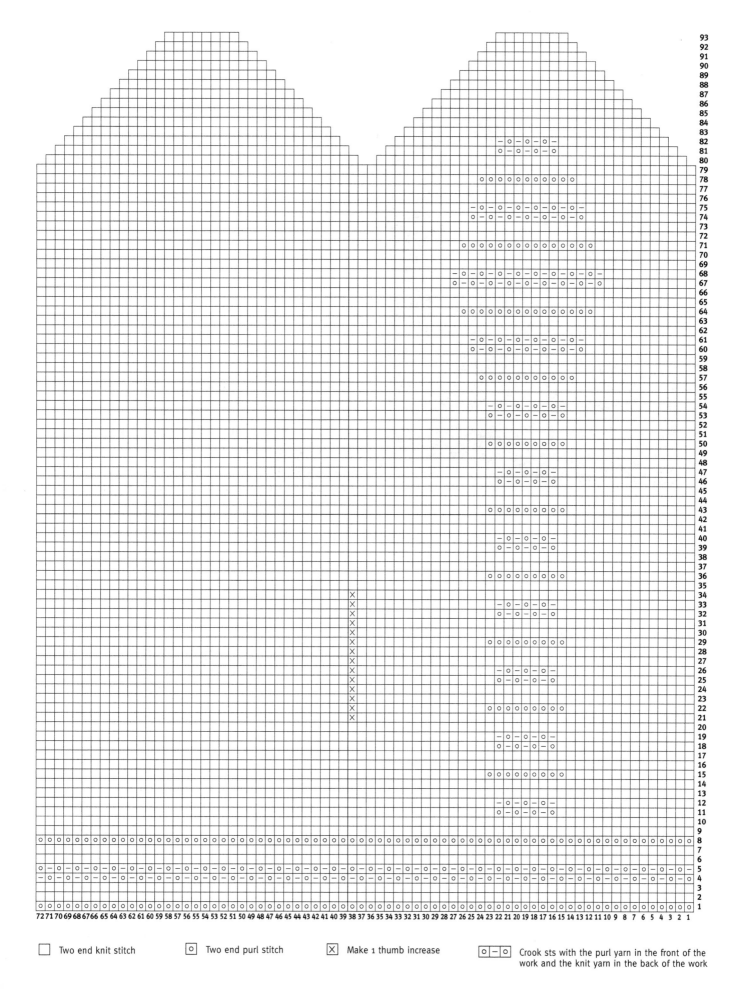

| | Two end knit stitch | | Two end purl stitch | | Make 1 thumb increase | | Crook sts with the purl yarn in the front of the work and the knit yarn in the back of the work |

129

RATATOSK* (TRYM)

by Elsebeth Lavold

Anders Rydell, photographer

Gauge

- 17 sts x 24 rows in pattern = 4 x 4 in / 10 x 10 cm

Materials

- 200 g Original yarn Elsebeth Lavold Designer's Choice ClassicAl
- Any wool or wool blend 4-ply yarn 50 g = 100 m
- US size 7 needles / 4.5 mm. Adjust needle size to obtain gauge if necessary.
- Cable needle

Size

Women's

Note: Worked without edge stitches; the first and last sts of the pattern are used for seaming.

Cap

Cast on 98 sts and knit 1 row, purl 1 row, knit 1 row for the edging.

Next row, RS: Work pattern rows 1–4 and then rows 1+2.

Place motifs

Work *14 sts in pattern, 14 sts from chart, repeat from * twice and end with 14 sts in pattern. After completing charted rows, work rows 1–4 5 times and end with Row 1. *Note: The 14 stitches in pattern are worked from Pattern Rows 1–4 below.*

Prepare for crown

Purl 1 row, knit 1 row), purl 1 row = 3 rows in reverse stockinette.

Crown

Now work stockinette. Place markers to divide the piece into 6 sections of 16 sts each + a seam stitch at beginning and end of row.

Decrease row

K1, *ssk, knit to 2 sts before marker, k2tog; repeat from * across row and end with k1. Decrease the same way on, alternately, every other and every 4th row until 14 sts remain. Cut yarn (leaving a tail of about 9¾ in / 25 cm) and pull tail through remaining sts. Seam center back and crown by grafting inside the seam stitches.

Mittens

Left mitten

Cast on 34 sts and knit 1 row, purl 1 row, knit 1 row for the edging.

Next row, RS: Begin working in pattern. After 2 repeats, work rows 1 and 2 and then, on the next RS row, begin thumb gusset: Work 17 sts, LLI, RLI and then complete row. Work 3 rows in pattern, keeping the new sts for the thumb gusset in stockinette.

Next row: work 17 sts, LLI, k2, RLI and complete row. Work 3 rows. Continue increasing the same way at each side within the 17 sts on every 4th row (there are 2 more sts between increases each time) until thumb gusset has 14 sts.

At the same time, after 6 pattern repeats, work rows 1 and 2 and then work charted motif. Place the motif between the sts for the thumb gusset and the last 2 sts on the row. Do not cut yarn.

Thumb

Using a new strand of yarn, work 6 rows in stockinette over the 14 sts for thumb.

Next row: K1, *ssk, work until 3 sts remain, k2tog, k1. Work another 7 rows. K2tog across and then cut yarn and pull tail through remaining sts.

Hand

Continue as set, picking up and knitting 2 new sts over thumb hole (in the 2 outermost sts of thumb). After completing charted motif, end by repeating the pattern 3 (4) times.

Shape top on RS rows: K1, *ssk, work to 2 sts before the center, k2tog; repeat from * and end with k1. Repeat the decreases on every other row until 14 sts remain. Cut yarn (leaving a tail of about 9¾ in/25 cm) and pull tail through remaining sts. Sew thumb and side seams, grafting inside the seam stitches.

Right mitten

Work as for left mitten, but the motif is placed between the first 2 sts and the thumb gusset.

PATTERN ROWS 1–4

Row 1: Knit

Row 2: purl

Row 3: *K2, p2; repeat from * and end with k2.

Row 4: *P2, k2; repeat from * and end with p2.

Repeat these 4 rows.

* **Editor's Note:** In Norse mythology, Ratatoskr (literally rat tusk) is a squirrel who runs up and down the world tree Yggdrasil to carry messages between the eagle at the top and a serpent who lives beneath the tree roots. There are two theories about his purpose—one is that gnawing at the tree is furthering the cycle of destruction and rebirth. The other (less flattering) is that this creature carries nasty gossip between the creatures at the top and bottom of the tree to provoke them.

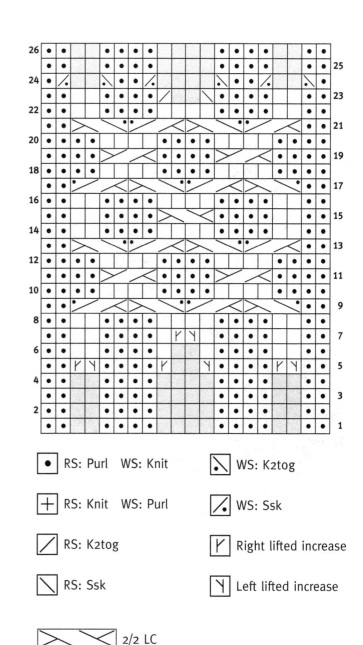

●	RS: Purl WS: Knit
+	RS: Knit WS: Purl
╱	RS: K2tog
╲	RS: Ssk
╲.	WS: K2tog
╱.	WS: Ssk
Γ	Right lifted increase
Ⅎ	Left lifted increase

2/2 LC

2/2 LpC

2/2 RC

2/2 RpC

▲ *Mittens adapted from Nordiska museet Gotland Mittens*

SW photo

▲ *Late 19th/early 20th century mittens from Gotland Island*

Courtesy of the Nordiska museet (NM.0116200a-b), Mona-Lisa Djerf, photographer

SUN WHEEL MITTENS

By Sara J Wolf

This mitten features a pattern typical on Gotland Island. The design references the sun wheel or sun-cross (wheel of life), frequently seen on Viking carved stones.

The source of the knitting pattern is a pair of mittens in the collection of the Nordiska museet from the late 19th/early 20th century. The mitten is very tightly worked in a yarn that produced 9 stitches/inch (although the yarn itself is a sport-weight that you'd expect to produce about 6 stitches/inch on a size 3 (3.25mm) needle. To achieve a gauge close to the original this example was knit on two US 0 (2.0mm) circular needles.

The original mittens were worked with the sun-cross pattern on the face of the thumb and a checkerboard pattern on the underside. With the slight difference in gauge using contemporary, commercially available yarn, the thumb placement did not occur in exactly the same location as on the historic example, so was simplified to use only the checkerboard design.

◄ *Sun Wheel (sun-cross) picture stone from the Gotland Museum*

SW photo

◁ *Chart B: Mitten Body Pattern*
(22 stitch repeat; 22 rows)

MC

CC

No stitch

133

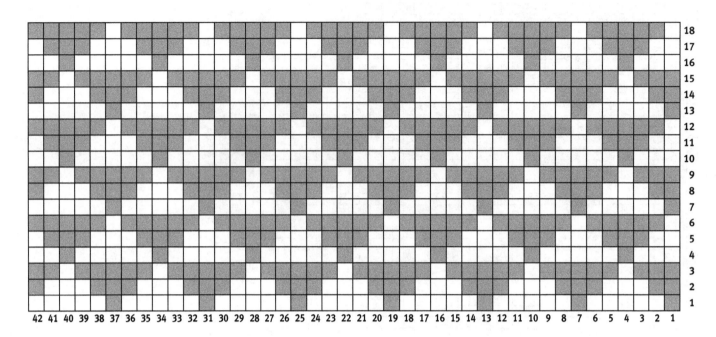

A Chart A: Mitten Cuff Pattern
  (6 stitch repeat; 18 rows)

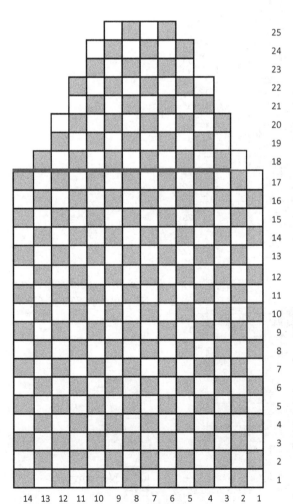

◄ Chart C: Thumb

Materials

- Kampes 2-ply wool, natural and brown (1 skein/ea)
- 2 US #0 (2.0mm) circular needles; one set US#0 (2.0mm) double-point needles
- smooth waste yarn (such as cotton) in a contrasting color
- tapestry needle
- stitch markers (optional)

Instructions

Using both yarns and the long-tail method, cast on 84 stitches (42 stitches on each needle) and join to work in the round.

Purl one round (dark).

Purl one round (light).

Mitten Cuff

Work Chart A for 18 rows.

Knit one row with the light color yarn, increasing 4 stitches evenly in the round (88 stitches).

Knit one more row with the light color and then begin Chart B.

Mitten Body

Following Chart B, work 22 rows.

For Left Mitten

Work the first 2 stitches of row 23. Knit the next 13 stitches with waste yarn. Return the stitches to the left needle and work in pattern for the remainder of row 23.

For Right Mitten

Work row 23 across needle 1 (2 pattern repeats). Work the first 2 stitches of needle 2. Knit the next 13 stitches with waste yarn. Return the stitches to the left needle and work in pattern for the remainder of row 23.

For both mittens, continue working in pattern through row 64.

Decrease rows

Beginning with row 65, k2together at the beginning and end of both needles (4 stitches decreased each row). Note: The first and last stitch shown on each row are shown as the stitch as worked together using the light or dark color of yarn that is used as the working yarn.

Continue decrease rows through row 81 (20 sts remaining). Break yarn, leaving a tail of at least 6". Thread a tapestry needle with the yarn tail and draw it through the remaining stitched, pulling the top together to close.

Bring the yarn tail through the top stitches again to secure and tighten, and bring the tail to the inside of the mitten. Secure the tail by weaving through the back side of the stitches.

Thumb

Remove waste yarn and place 13 stitches from each side of the gap on two double-point needles (4 needles total). Pick up 1 additional stitch from each side of the gap (14 stitches on each side; total of 28 stitches).

Attach both yarns (leaving a tail of at least 6") and work rounds alternating colors to form a checkerboard pattern. Begin decrease rows after completing row 17.

Decrease as follows

Work to the last stitch on needle 2. Knit the last stitch of needle 2 together with the first stitch of needle 3.

Work to the last stitch on needle 4. Knit the last stitch of needle 4 together with the first stitch of needle 1. One round completed, 2 stitches decreased.

Repeat decrease on row 19, 21, 23 and 25 (knit without decreasing on the even numbered rows 20, 22, and 24).

Break yarn after completing row 25, leaving a tail of at least 6". Thread a tapestry needle with the tail and pull the yarn through the remaining stitches, pulling them together to close the hole. Bring the yarn to the inside and fasten off by weaving through the back side of the stitches.

Thread the yarn tail from the point where you attached it to begin working the thumb onto a tapestry needle. If necessary, tighten up the stitches at the base of the thumb to close any gaps by working the tail thread through the backs of the stitches on the first row of the thumb. Fasten off the tails by weaving them through the back side of several stitches.

Finishing

Thread tails from the cast-on edge onto a tapestry needle and secure through the back side of stitches on the mitten interior.

Soak the mitten in warm water with a wool wash. Squeeze out excess water and shape to dry.

Editor's note: It is said that inserting a mistake in something hand-made will appease the gods who don't believe that anything should be perfect. That has never been a problem for me as you'll see looking at the sample mittens I knit. I used the dark color on one to separate the cuff from the body of the mitten, and the light color on the other. I guess that makes these fraternal rather than identical twins!

HERMANNA'S HAT

Adapted by Sara J Wolf

This pattern is based on a hat collected on Gotland Island by Hermanna Stengård around 1900. The original was knitted from very fine yarn that didn't match well to any of the current commercial brands, so there are some minor variations from the original

◁ Adaptation of Hermanna's Hat

Leah Nappi, model, Lauren Nappi, photographer

in this pattern. One difference is that when the knitter reached the decrease section a different, slightly thicker and fuzzier yarn was used. The knitter may just have run out of the original yarn, or this may have been a "design decision."

The hat features a hemmed brim with a simple stranded color work design, and the decrease rows form a lovely spiral.

The original red yarn was not dye fast, and when the hat became wet at some point, the red bled into the surrounding white. I wanted to make sure this didn't happen to my hat, so I tested the red yarn in warm, soapy water. A small amount of dye was visible, so before knitting, I soaked the yarn in water with a wool wash and small amount of vinegar to "set" the dye. This worked, but if it hadn't, I would have used a different yarn (something to keep in mind when you have two yarns with a strong contrasting color).

The hat shown on the model is the large size. I've provided the pattern in two sizes so that it also can be made to fit more snugly

Materials

- 1 skein Yllet Gotlands-garn 2 (white)
- 1 skein Yllet Gotlands-garn 2 (red or other contrasting color)
- Needles US 3 (3.25mm) 16" circular needle (or 5 dpns)
- US 2.5 (3.0mm) set of 5 dpns
- Stitch markers
- Yarn needle for weaving in ends
- Tape measure
- Usual knitting supplies

Instructions

Using the larger (circular) needle and white yarn, cast on 140 (150) stitches and join in the round. Mark the start of the round with a stitch marker.

Knit 6 rounds.

Purl 1 round. These 7 rounds will form a small hem.

Knit 2 rounds, then attach the contrasting color and work the chart.

After the final chart row, break the contrasting color yarn, leaving a tail of at least 6" to weave in later.

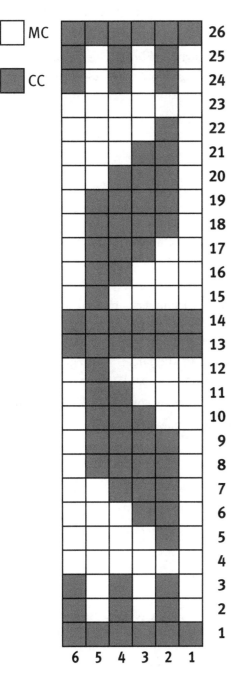

MC

CC

26
25
24
23
22
21
20
19
18
17
16
15
14
13
12
11
10
9
8
7
6
5
4
3
2
1

6 5 4 3 2 1

⋀ *Hermana's Hat Chart - 5 stitch repeat*

Continuing with the white yarn, knit one row, purl one row, and turn the work inside out.

Knit to the last 2 stitches of the round. Increase 1 stitch (KFB) and knit the last stitch. Remove the beginning-of-round stitch marker and slip the first stitch onto the right needle. Pull the last stitch knit on the right needle over the slipped stitch and drop it off the needle (like casting off). Replace the stitch marker. The beginning of the round has moved one stitch to the left, and the small hole made by turning the work should now be nearly invisible. The stitch count remains the same.

Work until the body of the hat is equal to the length of the brim (not including the hem), then work 2 more rounds.

Decrease Rows

For the small size: Knit one round with the smaller size double-point needles, placing 35 stitches on each of 4 needles. Make sure to mark the beginning of the round.

For the large size: Knit one round with the smaller size double-point needles, placing 30 stitches on each of 5 needles (you will need 6 dpns to work in this manner). Work 3 more rounds before beginning the decrease rows.

For both sizes: Work to the last 2 stitches on needle 1. Knit two stitches together (34 or 29 stitches remaining).

*Editor's Note: Using a smaller needle size for the decrease does not impact the size of the hat, but makes the spiral a little firmer. This causes it to stand out prominently on the crown.

Repeat for each of the other needles (1 stitch decreased on each needle).

Continue to decrease 1 stitch at the end of each needle on every row until 1 stitch remains on each needle (4

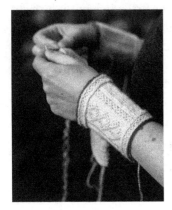

stitches for the small hat, 5 stitches for the large hat). Break the yarn leaving a tail of at least 6 inches. Pull the yarn through the remaining stitches to close the hole at the top. Take the yarn to the inside and fasten off the end by weaving in the end.

Wash and block the hat, folding along the purl rows to form the hem and the brim. When the hat is dry, weave in all remaining ends. With good blocking it should not be necessary to stitch down the starting hem. However, if you find that it curls out, tack the hem down with a minimum of stitches, taking care not to pull too tightly.

WOOL JOURNEY

by Josefin Waltin

Wool journey wrist warmers

I have a wool traveling club together with four spinning friends. We save money individually each month and once a year we make a wool journey together. We take an existing class or hire a teacher who can customize a course just for us. On the 2020 wool journey we hired Karin Kahnlund, master knitter and knitting teacher specializing in tvåändsstickning, two-end knitting (also referred to as twined knitting). In the course I made a pair of simple wrist warmers from traditional crook stitch patterns.

The finished circumference is 18 cm and fit my 21 cm hands nicely. If you want to alter the circumference of the wrist warmers you can add or delete in the knit sections on each end of the chain path ladders. If you want the wrist warmers longer or shorter you can add chain path rounds in the borders. If you want to make them longer

you may need to add shaping to compensate for the shape of the arm.

This pattern requires you to know twined knitting basics. If you don't, you can check out these resources (reference, including Spin-Off fall 2019).

Gauge

36 sts and 36 rounds = 10 cm square in twined stockinette using 2 mm needles

Measurements

18 cm circumference, 10 cm high. 3 cm negative ease.

Materials

- 50 g of Wålstedts Ullspinneri z-plied yarn in natural white. You can of course substitute the yarn with your own handspun. It needs to be z-ply, otherwise the structure will be off. The yarn will also get increasingly over twisted, making it difficult to knit.
- Scrap yarn in contrasting color for CO and BO edges
- 2 x 2.0 mm cable needles or 2 sets of 2.0mm dpns

Skills required

- Two-end knitting CO
- Two-end knitting knit stitches
- Two-end knitting purl stitches
- Crook stitches
- Two-end knitting BO

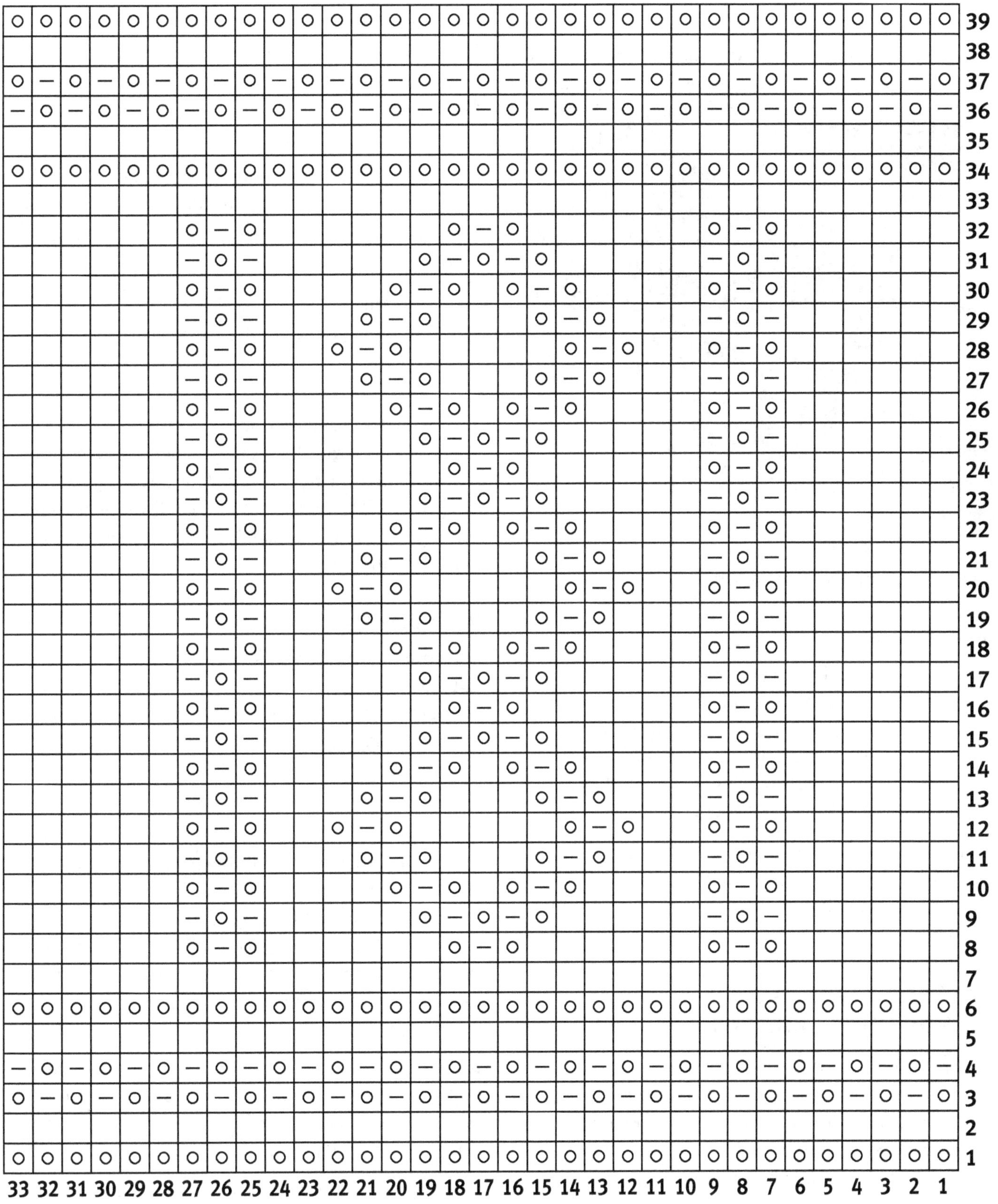

- (blank square) Two end knit stitch
- (o) Two end purl stitch
- (o – o) Crook sts with the purl yarn in the front of the work and the knit yarn in the back of the work

Pattern notes

The wrist warmers are knit as straight tubes in the round with identical front and back. I strongly recommend knitting both wrist warmers at the same time. This will

SW photo

save you the disaster of two different sizes.

Instructions

With your two-end knitting cast-on method of choice, CO 66 stitches with your two MC ends and one end of contrasting color scrap yarn. Leave 25 cm tails in the beginning for braiding or making a lanyard (correct word?). Cut scrap yarn, leaving 25 cm for braiding or lanyard. Join for working in the round.

Work in pattern for front of work, repeat for back of work. Work rounds 1–39. Cut MC yarn. Join two ends of scrap yarn and BO in two-end knitting. Weave in ends. Braid the CO ends or make lanyards.

VATTENBARVANTAR (CANDY DOT THRUMMED MITTENS)

by Sara J Wolf

Thrums are the threads left on a loom after the fabric has been cut off. For more than 400 years, knitters in Newfoundland, Labrador, England and Scandinavia have been incorporating thrums into mittens, socks, and hats to add insulation and warmth. These days, you are more likely to see mittens made with roving for the insulation. Though not technically thrums, the roving is soft and easy to manipulate, and makes a comfy lining. Using multi-colored roving produces a festive look that

reminds me of the penny candies that came on paper sheets I used to enjoy as a child.

Materials

- Worsted-weight yarn (e.g., Cascade 220)
- Size #4 US (3.5 mm) double point needles [Note: these mittens can be knit using the Magic Loop technique]
- 1-3 oz roving (dyed or plain)
- Tapestry needle
- Waste yarn
- Small crochet hook

Gauge

Approximately 6 stitches/inch in mitten body. These mittens are knit to a tight gauge using needles that are smaller than those typically used for this weight of yarn. The gauge will be influenced by the thickness and number of thrums in the mitten. Knit to fit the hand rather than a specific gauge.

Pattern Notes

This pattern is written for knitters using the "English style" of knitting—i.e., the working yarn is carried in the right hand. If you knit with the yarn in your left hand, the thrum will not stay in place if you "scoop" the working yarn to make the stitch. Adjust your technique to wrap the yarn under and then over the needle for the thrum stitches.

When you have finished knitting the mittens, you can adjust the thrums so that they sit slightly higher than the surface of the mitten by gently inserting a needle or crochet hook under the two legs of the thrum and very slightly loosening the fiber. This technique also can be used if a leg of the thrum has gotten pulled under the working yarn.

If you need to add (or replace worn) thrums after the mitten is complete, simply pull the thrum out with a crochet hook. Make a new thrum and work it into the stitch using the "duplicate stitch" technique.

These mittens are symmetrical, so they are neither left nor right. Both mittens are worked exactly the same.

Instructions

Cast on 36 stitches and arrange on 3 needles. Join in the round, marking the beginning of the round, and work 20 rounds of K2, P2 ribbing.

Round 21: *K2, m1, rep from * (54 sts)

Rounds 22-26 (5 rounds): Knit

Round 27: *K5, thrum, rep from * [Thrum row A]

Round 28: *K5, knit thrum tbl, rep from *

Rounds 29-32 (4 rounds): Knit

Round 33: K2, thrum, *K5, thrum.* Repeat from * to * to 3 sts before the end of the round. Knit the last 3 sts. [Thrum row B]

Round 34: Knit all stitches, knitting thrums tbl.

Rounds 35–36 (2 rounds): knit all stitches.

Round 37: Using a smooth waste yarn (such as cotton) in a contrasting color, knit across 6 stitches. Slide these stitches back onto the left needle and knit the entire round using the working yarn.

Round 38: knit all stitches

Continue knitting the thrum rounds as follows until the mitten is about ½" shorter than the length of your hand, ending just before a thrum row:

Round 39: *knit 5, thrum*, repeat from * to * to the end of the round.

Round 40: *knit 5, knit thrum tbl*; repeat from * to * to the end of the round.

Rounds 41–44: knit all stitches

Round 45: K2, thrum. *K5, thrum*; repeat * to * the end of the round.

Round 46: k2, k1tbl, *k5, k1tbl*; repeat * to * to last 3 stitches. K3.

Rounds 47–50 (4 rounds): knit.

Repeat 39–50 until the appropriate length is reached, ending just before a thrum row.

Top of Mitten (Decrease Rounds)

Work thrum row (use Thrum Round A round 27 if you have just finished round 50 or Thrum Round B if you have just finished round 44)

Next round: Knit all stitches, knitting thrums tbl.

Next round: *k2, k2tog*; repeat from * to * to the end of the row

Next round: *K1, k2tog*; repeat from * to * to the end of the row

Next round: *k2tog* repeat from * to * to the end of the row.

Break yarn, leaving at least a 6" tail. Thread tail onto a darning needle and run the tail through the remaining stitches on the needles. Remove the knitting needles and pull the stitches together to close the hole.

Bring the tail through to the inside of the mitten. As you fasten off and weave in the end of the tail, attach a large thrum to the mitten right under the hole.

Afterthought Thumb

With the cuff of the mitten facing you, pick up the **right side** of the stitches below the waste yarn.

Turn the mitten so that the cuff is facing away from you. With a second needle, pick up the **left side** of the stitches below the waste yarn.

Turn the mitten back so that the cuff is facing you, and attach the working yarn to begin knitting the stitches on needle 1, leaving a tail 6-8" long to weave in later. With an empty needle, knit 4 stitches from needle 1.

With another empty needle knit the remaining two stitches from needle 1 and pick up and knit 2 stitches from the gap (4 stitches each on needles 1 and 2).

Using another empty needle, k all stitches from the next needle, then pick up and knit 2 stitches from the gap. You should now have a total of 16 stitches for the thumb.

Knit 3 rounds

Round 4: Knit the round working thrums into stitch 3 on needle 1 and on needle 3.

Round 5: Knit all stitches, knitting thrums tbl.

Rounds 6–8 (3 rounds): knit.

Round 9: Knit the round working thrums into stitch 3 on needle 2 and stitch 7 on needle 3.

Round 10: Same as round 5.

Rounds 11–13: knit.

Continue working rounds 4–13 until you reach the crown of your thumb (it should barely show beyond the knitting).

Thumb Decreases:

Round 1: *K2 tog*; repeat from *to * to the end of the round (8 stitches remaining)

Round 2: *K2tog*; repeat from * to * to the end of the round (4 stitches remaining).

Break yarn leaving a 6–8: tail. Thread tail onto a darning needle and draw the tail through the remaining 4 stitches. Remove needles, pull the yarn tightly to close the hold, and thread the yarn to the inside. Before weaving in the end, fasten a large thrum into the top of the thumb right under the hole.

Finishing

Turn the mitten inside-out. Thread the tail of the yarn from the base of the thumb onto a darning needle and weave in the end, working around the base of the thumb to tighten any loose or stretched stitches and to close any remaining holes. When the tail has been secured, reduce the length of the tail to about 3" and unply the yarn so that it can act as an additional thrum.

Secure the end of the yarn from the cast-on edge by working it into the backs of the ribbing stitches (on the interior).

With the mitten still turned inside-out, gently wash in warm water with a little wool wash. Roll in a towel to remove some of the excess water and set out to dry. Drying over a drinking glass can help retain the shape.

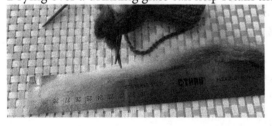

When dry, fluff out the thrums, turn right-side out again

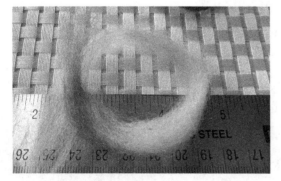

and you're finished…..except you need to…..

Make the second mitten.

Making Thrums

Materials

- Soft singles yarn or roving (dyed or plain)
- Ruler (optional)

Note: These instructions are written for working with the yarn in the right hand (aka English-style knitting). In order to fasten the thrum in place, you need to make

the stitch by bringing the working yarn from below the needle and around counter-clockwise.

Instructions

1. Pull out lengths of fiber about 6" in length.

2. Form a circle, overlapping the ends.

3. Felt the ends together by rubbing between your thumb and first finger (you can moisten your fingers to create a stronger felt).

Knitting in Thrums

4. Insert your needle into the stitch where you will place the thrum, then lay the folded thrum over the needle.

5. Wrap the working yarn around the needle to make a stitch.

6. Pull the loop through the stitch and thrum on the needle. You will see the stitch you just made sitting just to the left of the thrum.

7. Finish that round, working in thrums.

8. The next row fastens the thrum in place. Work to the thrum. Knit through the back loop (TBL) of the thrum and stitch. Working through the back loop causes the thrum to twist, making the characteristic heart or "v" shape on the outside of the mitten fabric. Note: You may need to tug slightly on the thrum if it sits up too high on the face of the mitten. You also can replace a thrum if it wears out by using a crochet hook to pull out the damaged thrum from inside the mitten, and then using the duplicate stitch technique, pull a new thrum into place.

The link below is a good article on how to work the duplicate stitch. This technique is also helpful to correct mistakes in stranded knitting.

*https://www.interweave.com/article/knitting/
duplicate-stitch-magic/*

POLSTJÄRNAN HEADBAND (POLARIS)

by Sara J Wolf

Description: This simple star pattern is found throughout Scandinavia. The first is a small border pattern of 11 rows, but you might also choose to adapt the 27 row Norrbotten Star for a wider band. Both charts are given (see notes at the end of the pattern.)

Materials

- Two contrasting colors of Wålstedts Tråändsgarn Nr 4, 7/2 yarn (less than 50g each)
- US #3 (3.25mm) 16" (40mm) circular needle
- Tapestry needle for weaving in ends.
- Stitch markers (optional)

Instructions for the Polstjärnan Headband

Using both colors of yarn and the long-tail method, cast on 144 stitches.

Join in the round, being careful not to twist the stitches, and place a marker to indicate the start of the round.

Work the 27 rows of the pattern.

Notes: The first and last row are a knit row of the light color only. Rows 2–4 and 24–26 are K2, P2 ribbing. Work the light color as knit stitches and the dark color as purl stitches.

Bind off with the dark color only.

Break yarns, leaving a tail of at least 6". Thread each tail into the darning needle and weave into the back side of the stitches to secure. Repeat with the tails left from the cast-on edge.

Soak in warm water with a wool wash. Squeeze out the excess water and block to dry.

Note: if you are at all concerned about dye fastness, steam block rather than wet block the piece. Alternatively, soak the dark color in a weak vinegar solution in water, rinse and dry before beginning to knit the headband.

Notes on Adapting the Norrbotten Star*:

The Norrbotten Star pattern is 28 stitches wide and 27 rows high, leaving 1 stitch between each repeat.

Cast on 140 stitches (5 star repeats) using both colors and the 2-color long-tail method as above.

Work rows 1–8 of the Polstjärnan chart as shown.

Work the 27 rows of the Norrbotten star chart.

Work rows 20–27 of the Polstjärnan chart as shown.

Bind off with the dark color only.

Break yarns, leaving a tail of at least 6". Thread each tail into the darning needle and weave into the back side of the stitches to secure. Repeat with the tails left from the cast-on edge.

Soak in warm water with a wool wash. Squeeze out the excess water and block to dry. [Note: if you are at all concerned about dye fastness, steam block rather than wet block the piece. Alternatively, soak the dark color in a weak vinegar solution in water, rinse and dry before beginning to knit the headband].

* The Norbotten star design is adapted from Solveig Larsson's book *Knitted Mittens*.

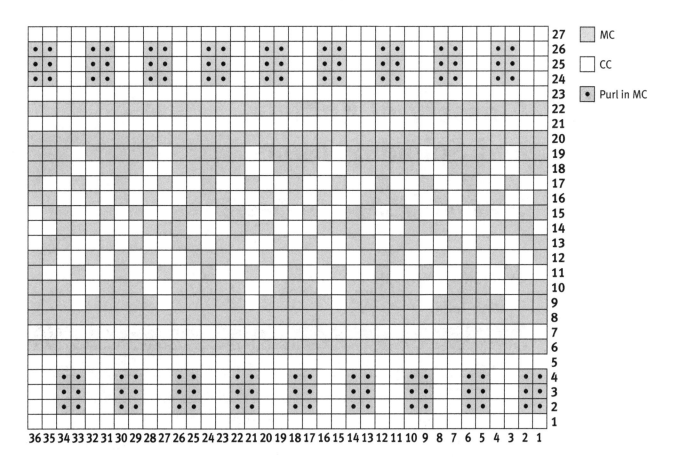

Legend:
- MC (shaded)
- CC (white)
- • Purl in MC

Row numbers (right): 27, 26, 25, 24, 23, 22, 21, 20, 19, 18, 17, 16, 15, 14, 13, 12, 11, 10, 9, 8, 7, 6, 5, 4, 3, 2, 1

Column numbers (bottom): 36 35 34 33 32 31 30 29 28 27 26 25 24 23 22 21 20 19 18 17 16 15 14 13 12 11 10 9 8 7 6 5 4 3 2 1

⋏ *Polstjärnan Chart*

⋎ *Norrbotten Star Chart*

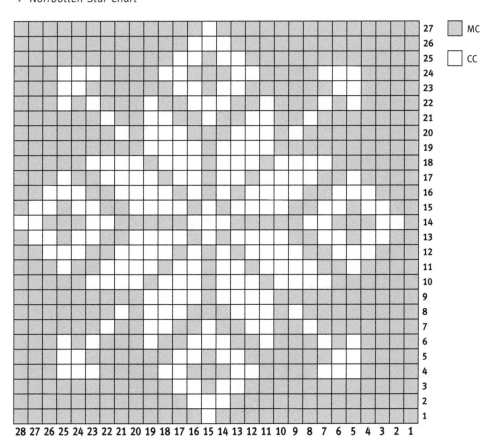

Legend:
- MC (shaded)
- CC (white)

Row numbers (right): 27, 26, 25, 24, 23, 22, 21, 20, 19, 18, 17, 16, 15, 14, 13, 12, 11, 10, 9, 8, 7, 6, 5, 4, 3, 2, 1

Column numbers (bottom): 28 27 26 25 24 23 22 21 20 19 18 17 16 15 14 13 12 11 10 9 8 7 6 5 4 3 2 1

145

8 Glossary of Knitting and Spinning Terms

Swedish/English-English/Swedish

SVENSKA/ENGLISH

Knitting Terms

STITCHES	
Svenska	**English**
avig maska (am)	purl stitch (p)
bakersta maskbågen	back loop
bakifrån, in i maskan	through the back of the loop (tbl)
beskrivning	description
bubbla	bobble
drag den lyfta m over	pass slipped stitch over (psso)
fläta	cable
främre maskbåge	front loop
maska (m)	stitch (st)
maskbåge/ögla	loop
moss-stickning	moss stitch
räta varv	knit row
rätmaska (rm)	knit stitch (k)
rätstickning	garter stitch
resårstickning	ribbed knitting
slätst med avigan ut	reverse stockinette
slätstickning/släst	stockinette stitch (St st)
smygmaska (sm)	slip stitch (sl st)
spets	lace
stygen	stitch
virka	crochet
vriden maska	twisted or crossed stitch

GARMENT TERMS

Svenska	English
ärm	arm/sleeve
ärmhål	armhole/armscye
ärmkulle	top shaping
axel	shoulder
axelsöm	shoulder seam
bakstycke	back
bål	body
bård	border
fåll	hem
ficka	pocket
forma ärmkullen	shoulder shaping
framkant	front band/edge
framsidan (på arb)	front side/right side (RS)
framstycke	front piece
halskant	neckband
hel längd	complete length
halsringning	neckline
höfter	hips
höger framst	right front
kant	edge
kjol	skirt
klänning	dress
knappar	buttons
knapphål	buttonhole
knapphålskant	front band with buttonholes

GARMENT TERMS (con't.)

Svenska	English
kofta	cardigan
krage	collar
luva	cap/hood
mittstycke	center front/back
mössa	hat
mudd, manschett	cuff
nederkant	hem
ok	yoke
öppning	opening
övervidd, bröstmått	chest measurement
ränder	stripes
resår	rib
polokrage	turtleneck
runt ok	yoke (knit in the round)
sjal	scarf
sockor	socks
söm	seam
spets	lace
storiek	size
tröja	pullover
vante	mitten
vänster framst	left front
väst/linne	vest
veck	pleat
vik	fold

YARN

Svenska	English
akryl	acrylic
alpacka	alpaca
bomull	cotton
brodergarn	embroidery yarn
kamgarn	worsted
kardgarn	woolen
Kedjetvina	chain ply
enträdigt	single
garn, tråd	yarn
härva	skein
lin	linen
nystan	ball
S-tvinnat	S-plied
silke	silk
tretrådig	3-ply
tvåradig	2-ply
ull	wool
Z-tvinnat	Z-plied

EQUIPMENT

Svenska	English
flätsticka/ hjälpsticka (hj.st)	cable needle (cn)
höger sticka	right needle
knappar	buttons
markör märktråd	marker (m)
märktråd	waste yarn
maskhållare	stitch holder
mönster	pattern
nystapinne	nostepinne
nystmaskin	ball winder
rundsticka	circular needle
sticka	knit, needle, knitting needle
strumpstickor	double pointed needles (dpn)
virknål	crochet hook
valkbräde	fulling/felting board

WEIGHTS AND MEASURES

Svenska	English
1 cm = 0.39 in	1 inch (in) = 2,54 cm
bystvidd	chest measurement
en	one
mäta	measure
mätt	measurement
övervidd/bröstmått	chest measurement
på längden	lengthwise
pund (1oz=28,35 gr)	ounces (oz) (1oz=29,35 g)
stickfasthet	gauge/tension
ungefär	approximately
viktmått (1lbs=456gr)	pound (lbs)

INSTRUCTIONS	
Svenska	*English*
alla	every
allt	all
alltid	always
andra, 2:a	second
återstående	remaining
avigsidan	wrong side (WS)
avmaska av	bind off
avsluta	finishing
bara	only
börja/början	begin/beginning
byt	change
byt mellan	alternate (alt)
cirka (ca)	approximately (approx.)
de stickade maskorna	stitches used
dela	divide
dela på mitten	divide at the center
delbart med	work a multiple of
drag den lyfta m over	pass slipped stitch over (psso)
eller	or
en	one
endast	only
flera	multiple (mult)
flytta	transfer
flytta markören	slip marker (sm)
fördelat på 4 strumpst	divide on 4 double point needles
föregående	previous
föregående varv	previous row
förklaring/förkl	explanation
form	shape

INSTRUCTIONS (con't.)	
Svenska	*English*
först	first
fortsätt	continue
förutom	except
främre maskbåge	front loop
från *-*	from * to *
gånger gr	times
garnet bakom	yarn behind
garnet framför arb	yarn over/yarn forward
genom	through
genom främre maskbågen	through front loop (tfl)
höger	right
hoppa över	skip/pass over/miss
hoppa over en maska	skip a stitch
ihop, tillsamans, tills	together (tog)
inåt	inward
inklusive	including
intagning	decreasing
jämnt	even
klipp tråden	fasten off
kvar	remaining
lägg upp	cast on (CO)
längd	length
längs med	lengthwise
lyft 1 m	slip 1 stitch (sl 1)
lyft 1 rm	slip 1 knitwise (sl 1 kw)
märktråd	marking thread/waste yarn
maska av (avm)	bind off (BO)
mäta	measure
mått	measurement
mellanrum	space

Svenska	English
minska	decrease
mitten	center
mittmaskan	central stitch
mönsterrapport	pattern repeat
montering	join
motsatt sida	opposite side
nästa	following
också	also
ojämna antal varv	odd number of rows
ojämnt antal maskor	odd number of stitches
öka/ökning	increase
omslag	yarn over (YO)
omvänt	reverse
placera	place
plocka upp	pick up
runt	round
så här	like this
samma	same
samtidigt	at the same time
sätt I en markör	place marker (pm)
sätt ihop/sätt samman	join
sätt maskorna på en hjälpsticka	place on stitch holder
sedan	then
sista	last
smygmaska (sm)	slip stitch (sl st)
som	as
spegelvänd	mirrored
sprund	split

Svenska	English
sticka I bakre maskbågen	knit into the back loop (kbl)
sticka rakt upp/sticka upp maskor	work even
sticka runt	knit in the round
sticka tillbaka	work back
sträcka/töja sig	stretch
tappa en mask	drop a stitch
totalt	altogether
ungefär	approximately
upprepa dessa x varv	repeat these x rows
varv (v)	row, round
vänd arbetet, väand/vända	turn the work
vänster	left
var för sig	separate, separated
varannan	every other
varje	every/each
varv	row/round
varvantal	number of rows
varvhöjd	number of rows in length
växelvis	alternate (alt)
vidare	then
vik	fold

Examples

1rm, 1am	K1, P1
2rm, 2am	K2, P2
lyft 1 m	sl 1
sticka ihop 2 am	p2tog
sticka ihop 2 rm	k2tog

SPINNING TERMS

Svenska	English
dra fram	draft
enträdigt	single
fall	drape
härva	skein
kamband	combed top
kamgarn	worsted
kamma	comb (v)
karda	card
kardgarn	woolen
kardrulle	rolag
kedjetvinna	chain ply
klippände	cut end
korta drag	short draw
krus	crimp
långdrag	longdraw
nystan	(yarn) ball
pälsull/gobelängull	wool with mostly or only outercoat
S-tvinnat	S-plied
snodd	twist
spinnområde	drafting zone
spinntriangeln	drafting triangle
stapel	staple
täckull	outercoat
tesa	tease
tretrådig	3-ply
tvåradig	2-ply
toppände, topp	tip end
märghår, dödhår	kemp

Svenska	English
ull av finullstyp	wool with mostly or only undercoat
ull av ryatyp	wool with undercoat and outercoat
ull av vadmalstyp	wool with lots of undercoat and a few strands of outercoat

SPINNING EQUIPMENT

Svenska	English
fiberfäste	distaff
hängande slända	suspended spindle/drop spindle
härvträ	niddy-noddy
kam	card
kardmaskin	drum carder
Navajoslända, golvstödd slända	Navajo spindle
slända	spindle
spinnrock	spinning wheel
spolställ	lazy Kate
teskarda	flick card
understödd slända, stödd slända	supported spindle
valkbräde	fulling/felting board

ANIMALS

Svenska	English
bagge	ram
lamm	lamb
tacka	ewe

ENGLISH/SVENSKA

Knitting Terms

STITCHES	
English	*Svenska*
back loop	bakersta maskbågen
bobble	bubbla
cable	fläta
crochet	virka
description	beskrivning
front loop	främre maskbåge
garter stitch	rätstickning
knit row	räta varv
knit stitch (k)	rätmaska (rm)
lace	spets
loop	maskbåge/ögla
moss stitch	moss-stickning
pass slipped stitch over (psso)	drag den lyfta m over
purl stitch (p)	avig maska (am)
reverse stockinette	slätst med avigan ut
ribbed knitting	resårstickning
slip stitch (sl st)	smygmaska (sm)
stitch (st)	maska (m), stygen
stockinette stitch (St st)	slätstickning/släst
through the back of the loop (tbl)	bakifrån, in i maskan
twisted or crossed stitch	vriden maska

GARMENT TERMS	
English	*Svenska*
arm/sleeve	ärm
armhole/armscye	ärmhål
back	bakstycke
body	bål
border	bård
buttonhole	knapphål
buttons	knappar
cap/hood	luva
cardigan	kofta
center front/back	mittstycke
chest measurement	övervidd, bröstmått
collar	krage
complete length	hel längd
cuff	mudd, manschett
dress	klänning
edge	kant
fold	vik
front band/edge	framkant
front band with buttonholes	knapphålskant
front piece	framstycke
front side/right side (RS)	framsidan (på arb)
hat	mössa
hem	fall, nederkant
hips	höfter

GARMENT TERMS (con't.)	
English	*Svenska*
lace	spets
left front	vänster framst
mitten	vamte
neckband	halskant
neckline	halsringning
opening	öppning
pleat	veck
pocket	ficka
pullover (jumper)	tröja
rib	resår
right front	höger framst
scarf	sjal
seam	söm
shoulder	axel
shoulder seam	axelsöm
shoulder shaping	forma ärmkullen
size	storiek
skirt	kjol
socks	sockor
stripes	ränder
top shaping	ärmkulle
turtleneck	polokrage
vest	väst/linne
yoke (yoke knit in the round)	ok (runt ok)

YARN

English	Svenska
acrylic	akryl
alpaca	alpacka
ball	nystan
chain ply	kedjetvinna
cotton	bomull
embroidery yarn	brodergarn
linen	lin
S-plied	S-tvinnat
single	entrådigt
skein	härva
silk	silke
wool	ull
woolen	kardgarn
worsted	kamgarn
Z-plied	Z-tvinnat

EQUIPMENT

English	Svenska
ball winder	nystmaskin
buttons	knappar
cable needle	flätsticka/ hjälpsticka (hj.st)
circular needle	rundsticka
crochet hook	virknål
double pointed needles (dpn)	strumpstickor
fulling/felting board	valkbräde
knit, needle, knitting needle	sticka
marker (m)	markör märktråd
nostepinne	nystapinne
pattern	mönster
right needle	höger sticka
stitch holder	maskhållare
waste yarn	märktråd

WEIGHTS AND MEASURES

English	Svenska
1 inch (in) = 2,54 cm	1 cm = 0.39 in
approximately	ungefär
chest measurement	bystvidd, övervidd/ bröstmått
gauge/tension	stickfasthet
lengthwise	på längden
measure	mäta
measurement	mätt
one	en
ounces (oz) [1oz=29,35 g]	pund (1oz=28,35 gr)
pound (lbs)	viktmått (1lbs=456gr)

English	Svenska
all	allt
also	också
alternate (alt)	byt mellan/ växelvis
altogether	totalt
always	alltid
approximately (approx.)	cirka (ca)/ ungefär
as	som
begin/beginning	börja/början
bind off (BO)	avmaska av (avm)
cast on (CO)	lägg upp
center	mitten
central stitch	mittmasken
change	byt
continue	fortsätt
decrease	minska
decreasing	intagning
divide	dela
divide at the center	dela på mitten
divide on 4 double point needles	fördelat på 4 strumpst
drop a stitch	tappa en mask
even	jämnt
every	alla
except	förutom
explanation	förklaring/förkl
fasten off	klipp tråden
finishing	avsluta
first	först
fold	vik
following	nästa

English	Svenska
from * to *	från *-*
front loop	främre maskbåge
including	inklusive
increase	öka/ökning
inward	inåt
join	montering, sätt ihop/sätt samman
knit in the round	sticka runt
knit into the back loop (kbl)	sticka I bakre maskbågen
last	sista
length	längd
lengthwise	längs med
like this	så här
measure	mått
measurement	mellanrum
mirrored	spegelvänd
multiple (mult)	flera
number of rows	varvantal
odd number of rows	ojämna antal varv
number of rows in length	varvhöjd
odd number of stitches	ojämnt antal maskor
one	en
only	bara, endast
opposite side	motsatt sida
or	eller
pass slipped stitch over (psso)	drag den lyfta m over
pattern repeat	mönsterrapport
pick up	plocka upp
place	placera

English	Svenska
place marker (pm)	sätt I en markör
place on stitch holder	sätt maskorna på en hjälpsticka
previous	föregående
previous row	föregående varv
remaining	återstående, kvar
repeat these x rows	upprepa dessa x varv
reverse	omvänt
right	höger
round	runt
row/round	varv
same/at the same time	samma/ samtidigt
second	andra, 2:a
shape	form
skip/pass over/miss	hoppa över
skip a stitch	hoppa over en maska
slip marker (sm)	flytta markören
stitches used	de stickade maskorna
slip 1 stitch (sl 1)	lyft 1 m
slip 1 knitwise (sl 1 kw)	lyft 1 rm
slip stitch (sl st)	smygmaska (sm)
space	mellanrum
split	sprund
stretch	sträcka/töja sig
then	sedan/vidare
through	genom
through front loop (tfl)	genom främre maskbågen
times	gånger gr
together (tog)	ihop, tillsamans, tills
transfer	flytta

English	Svenska
waste yarn/marking thread	märktråd
work a multiple of	delbart med
work back	sticka tillbaka
work even	sticka rakt upp/sticka upp maskor
wrong side (WS)	avigsidan
yarn behind	garnet bakom
yarn over/yarn forward (YO)	garnet framför arb, omslag

Examples

K1, P1	1rm, 1am
K2, P2	2rm, 2am
k2tog	sticka ihop 2 am
p2tog	sticka ihop 2 am
sl 1	lyft 1 m

SPINNING

English	Svenska
2-ply	tvåradig
3-ply	tretrådig
ball	nystan
chain ply	kedjetvinna
combed top	kamband
crimp	krus
cut end	klippände
drafting triangle	spinntriangeln
drafting zone	spinnområde
drape	fall
felt/full	valka
from the fold	vikt
kemp	märghår, dödhår
longdraw	långdrag
outercoat	täckull
ratio	utväxling
rolag	kardrulle
S-plied	S-tvinnat
short draw	korta drag
single	entrådigt
skein	härva
staple	stapel
tease	tesa
tip end	toppände, topp
twist	snodd
undercoat	underull
wool with mostly or only outercoat	pälsull/gobelängull
wool with mostly or only undercoat	ull av finullstyp

SPINNING (con't.)

English	Svenska
wool with lots of undercoat and only a few strands of outercoat	ull av vadmalstyp
wool with undercoat and outercoat	ull av ryatyp
woolen	kardgarn
worsted	kamgarn
Z-plied	Z-tvinnat

SPINNING EQUIPMENT

English	Svenska
card	karda
comb	kamma
distaff	fiberfäste
drop spindle/suspended spindle	Hängande slända
drum carder	kardmaskin
felting/fulling board	valkbräde
flick card	teskarda
lazy Kate	spolställ
Navajo spindle	Navajoslända, golvstödd slända
niddy-noddy	härvträ
spindle	slända
spinning wheel	spinnrock
supported spindle	understödd slända, stödd slända

ANIMALS

English	Svenska
ewe	tacka
lamb	lamm
ram	bagge

9 Other Resources

There are quite a few rabbit holes to dive into in the search for Swedish yarn and fleece. We have connected web addresses for many of the mills and yarn companies, but there are a few other organizations you might want to check into from time to time if you are planning a trip or conducting more research of your own.

SWEDISH SHEEP/BREED ASSOCIATIONS

Föreningen Svenska Allmogefår

https://allmogefar.se/

This organization maintains the Gene Bank and official list of sheep breeds considered endangered or otherwise threatened. They provide good summaries of information on each of the listed breeds along with photographs of typical rams, ewes and lambs to help you identify the various types of sheep. Some of the entries also provide additional information on fiber micron size, the character of the yarn (e.g., rya vs. finull) and the traditional area in Sweden where the sheep were found.

Svenska Fåravelsförbundet

http://www.faravelsforbundet.se/

The Swedish Sheep Federation is a trade association for sheep farmers, shepherds and shepherdesses. Their purpose is to promote all aspects of sheep farming and the associated businesses. The website is large and deep with information on local associations, businesses and advertisements. They also post links to research projects, and have a Facebook page with loads of fun images.

Ullvilja

https://ullvilja.se/

Ullvilja is a non-profit membership association with the goal of promoting the use of Swedish wool. Annually they co-sponsor both a hand spinning and a fleece competition in the fall. The venue changes, but the event also includes a market and an auction of the fleece. It is the one event where hand spinners can interact with producers of the highest quality fleece in the country, and where they might even be able to take a prize-winner home. It also is an opportunity to network with many of the other spinners and shepherds/shepherdesses to develop long-term relationships and ongoing supplies of fleece.

FLEECE AND FIBER

Swedish Fibre

https://www.swedishfibre.com/

There are two sides to the Swedish Fibre site. First, the information on the rare breeds is one of the best places to begin to get your mind around the variety and complexity of the subject. The site is very well illustrated and the information succinct. The other side is their retail outlet via Etsy where you can locate some types of raw fleece and roving. Their selection is highly variable and seasonally dependent.

Ullförmedlingen

https://ullformedlingen.se/

In 2017 Fia Söderberg began a project to put together a digital marketplace for Swedish wool. It began with a Facebook page for buyers and sellers to "meet up" and ultimately to provide an arena to promote Swedish wool and reduce wool waste. Spending some time going through the marketplace is a very good way to begin to understand what is available across the country.

Ullförmedlingen is a free service, and a great place to find a good variety of fleece both from heritage breeds and more common types as well. Some producers also offer hand or mill-spun yarns from their farms. Availability for shipping outside of Sweden varies.

An important note on importing raw fleece to the US: There is no prohibition on importation of raw fleece from Sweden because it is not a country that has active Foot and Mouth Disease. That being said, individual customs agents may have questions for you. If you are having something mailed to you, ask the seller to include a note that states that the wool is from a healthy animal and an FMD-free country. While the fleece does not have to be washed, it should be free of feces and blood. The USDA website also has a table of regulatory actions about wool, hair and bristles that shows the agent that the fleece should be released if free of feces and blood (Table 3-10-11 and page 3-10-14), reproduced here.

Including a copy of this table in the shipment might help prevent problems if the customs agent is not familiar with fleece importation.

Other locations: There are very specific restrictions on import/export from Sweden to the EU and UK as well as other countries like Australia and New Zealand with large sheep populations. Check the customs and agricultural ministry regulations within your own country to determine the appropriate guidance for importing raw fleece and wool.

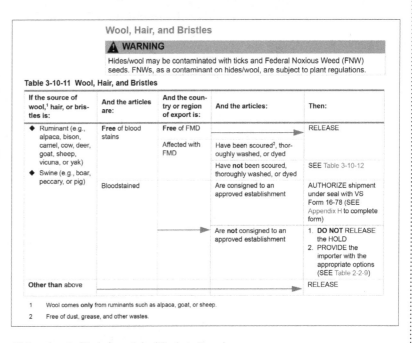

Wool, Hair, and Bristles

⚠ WARNING

Hides/wool may be contaminated with ticks and Federal Noxious Weed (FNW) seeds. FNWs, as a contaminant on hides/wool, are subject to plant regulations.

Table 3-10-11 Wool, Hair, and Bristles

If the source of wool,[1] hair, or bristles is:	And the articles are:	And the country or region of export is:	And the articles:	Then:
◆ Ruminant (e.g., alpaca, bison, camel, cow, deer, goat, sheep, vicuna, or yak)	Free of blood stains	Free of FMD		RELEASE
		Affected with FMD	Have been scoured[2], thoroughly washed, or dyed	
◆ Swine (e.g., boar, peccary, or pig)			Have **not** been scoured, thoroughly washed, or dyed	SEE Table 3-10-12
	Bloodstained		Are consigned to an approved establishment	AUTHORIZE shipment under seal with VS Form 16-78 (SEE Appendix H to complete form)
			Are **not** consigned to an approved establishment	1. **DO NOT RELEASE** the HOLD 2. PROVIDE the importer with the appropriate options (SEE Table 2-2-9)
Other than above				RELEASE

1 Wool comes **only** from ruminants such as alpaca, goat, or sheep.
2 Free of dust, grease, and other wastes.

US Department of Agriculture, Animal Products Manual

BIBLIOGRAPHY

Åberg, Erika. Sticka Vantar: socker och lite till. Sundbyberg, Bokförlaget Semic, 2016.

Åberg, Erika. Sticka varm och mönstrat. Sundbyberg, Bokförlaget Semic, 2018.

Allas, Karen and Anu Sepp, eds. Woolen Handicrafts on the Baltic Islands. Talin, Estonia, KnowSheep-project and the Estonian Crop Research Institute, 2013.

Andersson, Eva B. *Tools, Textile Production and Society in Viking Age Birka. In: Dressing the Past,* M. Glema et al, eds., Ancient Textiles Series 3, Oxford, Oxbow Books, 2008.

Arvidsson, Harry. Swedish Crafts and Craft Education, *Studies in Design Education Craft and Technology,* Vol. 21, no. 3, 1989. Pps 157-161.

Asplund, Ivar. Cable Knits from Nordic Lands. North Pomfret, VT, Trafalger Square Books, 2019 (translation of Sticka Flätor).

Asplund, Ivar. Sticka Flätor. Lettland, Livonia Print, 2017.

Carlsson, Eva. Hatt och vante funna I Faluns kulturlager. Dagsverket, No. 4, 2016, pp 12-13.

Dandanell, Birgitta, Ulla Danielsson and Kerstin Ankert. Tvåändsstickat. Falun, Sweden, Dalarnas museum, 2011.

Dandanell, Birgitta and Ulla Danielsson. Twined Knitting. Loveland, CO, Interweave Press, 1989.

Ejstrud, Bo, Stina Andresen, Amanda Appel, Sara Gjerlevsen and Birgit Thomsen. From Flax to Linen: Experiments with flax at Ribe Viking Centre. Esbjerg, Denmark, Maritime Archaeology Programme, University of Southern Denmark, 2011.

Falck, Erika Nordvall. Facy Mittens—Markkinavanthuit. Jokkmokk, Sweden, Ájtte, Svenskt fjäll—och samemuseum, 2018.

Flanders, Sue and Janine Kosel. Swedish Handknits.Minneapolis, MN, Voyageur Press, 2012.

Forte, Mary. Entrelac Knitting Lesson. *Cast On,* The Knitting Guild Association, August-October 2009, pp 30-36.

Gibson-Roberts, Priscilla A. and Deborah Robson. *Knitting in the Old Way.* Fort Collins, CO, Nomad Press, 2004.

Gottfridsson, Inger and Ingrid Gottfridsson. *The Mitten Book.* Asheville, NC, Lark Books, 1984.

Greenfieldboyce, Nell. "The Oldest String Ever Found May have been Made by Neanderthals," NPR Science, April 10, 2020.

Kahnlund, Karin. Center Blocks: Swedish Two-end Mittens. *PieceWork* Magazine, January/February 2011, pp 23-24

Kahnlund, Karin. Sticka efter Svenska Mönster. Stockholm, Bokförlaget Rediviva, 2011.

Kahnlund, Karin. Tvåändsstickning. Hemslöjdens förlag (Truck: Göteborgstryckeriet), 2019

Larsson, Marika. Stickat från Norrbotton. Stockholm, LTs förlag, 1978.

Larsson, Solveig. Knitted Mittens. North Pomfret, VT, Trafalger Square Books, 2015

Lavold, Elsebeth. *Viking Knits and Ancient Ornaments*. North Pomfret, VT, Trafalger Square Books, 2014.

Lavold, Elsebeth. Viking Patterns for Knitting. North Pomfret, VT, Trafalger Square Books, 2000 (© 1998 Elsebeth Lavold an ICAFörlager AB, Västerås)

Ling, Anne-Maj. Two-End Knitting. Pittsville, WI, Schoolhouse Press, 2004.

Mathiassen, Tove Engelhardt, Marie-Louise Nosch, Maj Ringgard, Kirsten Toftegaard and Mikkel Venbord Pederson, eds. Fashionable Encounters: Perspectives and Trends in Textile and Dress in the Early Modern Nordic World. Oxford & Philadelphia, Oxbow Books, 2014.

Mellgren, Nusse. Nålbindning. Klippan, Ljungbergs tryckeri, 2017.

Overland, Viveka. Bohus Stickning på nytt. Uddevalla, Bohusläns museums förlag, 2016.

Pagoldh, Suzanne. Nordic Knitting. Loveland, CO, Interweave Press, 1991 (translation of the 1987 edition from Anfang Publishers, Inc., Stockholm).

Rhodes, Carol Huebscher. Cuffs in two-End Knitting, *PieceWork* Magazine, January/February 2011, p,21-22.

Pink, Anu, Siiri Reimann and Kristi Jõeste. Estonian Knitting 1. Traditions and Techniques. Türi Estonia, Saara Publishing House, 2016

Pink, Anu. Estonian Knitting 2. Socks and Stockings. Türi Estonia, Saara Publishing House, 2018.

Rhodes, Carol Huebscher. Two-End Knitting: A Living Tradition. *PieceWork* Magazine, January/February 2011, p,19-21.

Ricketts, Laura. Beauties from the Far North: Swedish Sámi Knitted Mittens. E-book at *www.LauraRickettsDesigns.com*. Undated.

Ricketts, Laura. Discover the Wonderful World of Sami Knitting: 5 Mitten Patterns from Finland, Norway & Sweden to Knit. An e-Book from *PieceWork*, *www.needleworktraditions.com*. Undated

Robson, Deborah and Carol Ekarius. The Fleece and Fiber Sourcebook. North Adams, MA, Storey Publishing, 2011.

Rutt, Richard. A History of Hand Knitting. Loveland, CO, Interweave Press, 1987.

Sokalski, Linda D.Y. Swedish Two-strand Knitting. *Threads* Magazine, Newtown, CT, Taunton Press, Number 26, December 1898-January 1990, pp44-47.

Sokalski, Linda D.Y. Tvåändsstickning Mitten. *Threads* Magazine, Newtown, CT, Taunton Press, Number 26, December 1898-January 1990, p48.

Stengård, Hermanna. Gotländsk Sticksöm. Stockholm, Bokförlaget Rediviva (facsimile of the 1925 edition), 2014.

Tribe, Shawn. Pontifical Gloves: A Brief History and Consideration. *Liturgical Arts Journal*, 7/17/2018.

Turnau, Irena. History of Knitting Before Mass Production. Warsaw, Institute of the History of Material Culture, Polish Academy of Sciences, 1991.

Vessby, Malin. Dra På Trissor, *Hemslöjd*, No. I, 2020. Hemslöjden, pp22-27.

Waltin, Josefin. Sorting Fleeces: A Study in Gute and Gotland. *Spinn Off*, Fort Collins, CO, Interweave Press, Spring 2019.

Wintzell, Inga. Sticka mönster: Historisk om stickning I Sverge. Stockholm, Nordiska museet (Tryckt hos Bohusläningens AB, Uddevlla), 1980.

CPSIA information can be obtained
at www.ICGtesting.com
Printed in the USA
LVHW061454050321
680666LV00006B/71